BELIEVING BIGGER
A 31- DAY FAITH JOURNEY
By Dr. Shante Bishop

DEDICATION

This book is dedicated to Mandi – a wife, mom, and entrepreneur. Four days before I started writing Believing Bigger, Mandi called to tell me that she had been struggling with depression and that, for a time, she had lost her way. She said that as she tried to emerge from the fog, she began searching for something...a devotional that would speak to her spiritually and emotionally. She could not find one to meet her needs.

Mandi told me that as she prayed for direction, God told her that I had an answer and would write the devotional she needed. I ended that conversation with a polite acknowledgement that I hoped to do that, "someday."

Two days later, God told me in no uncertain terms to, *"Answer the Call!"* This book is a result of literally and figuratively answering that call.

SPECIAL THANKS

To God Always. To my family for putting up with me during this season of growth, for being an extra set of hands and loving caregivers for my child. To my launch team who lined up behind me, without hesitation and helped me to push. For everyone who prayed, believed, invested, and supported me. Thank you.

"I am OBSESSED with this book! Even the introduction was SO powerful! I absolutely love it!" – **Aisha Taylor**

"This book speaks volumes! If you are in a low state of mind, this book will definitely lift your spirits and change the way you think!" – **Lakia Griffin**

"I had to stop myself from reading it in one night! Dr. Shante is about to CHANGE LIVES! I can't wait to share this with my clients!" – **Dr. Tiffany Bellamy**

"...I should have read this in the privacy of my home. Train rides and restaurants are not the place for the full ugly cry. I was done from the first sentence." – **Tamika Brown**

"I've read so many devotionals that seem to merely tell me what I already know about scriptures I've already read a gazillion times and leave me without an action plan.

This managed to tug on my heart strings more than once, caused me to do some serious soul searching, and then gave me actionable steps to take next.

This was needed - for me and, I'm sure, for an unimaginable number of people stuck spiritually in "neutral".
I've read so many devotionals that seem to merely tell me what I already know about scriptures I've already read a gazillion times and leave me without an action plan. This managed to tug on my heart strings more than once, caused me to do some serious soul searching and gave me the actions to move forward. I cannot WAIT for others to read what I'm reading!– **Carla D. Brown**

" So grateful for the transparency in this book. Dr Shante gets it!"
– **Jhmira Latrice**

"Wow! Nothing short of phenomenal! I don't yet know what God is calling me to do, but this is the year that I answer the call!" – **Dionna Ford**

"This book hits so many nails on the head...I battle with perfectionism, but Dr. Shante is helping me to see that people are waiting on me to show up!" - **Courtney Powell**

"Dr. Shante is the TRUTH!" **Terry Connor**

"This is going to bless SO MANY lives!" **Dionna Ford**

"I used this as my devotion this morning and I was in tears...Can't wait to share this with others!" **Lisa Seymour**

Contents

INTRODUCTION

As an educator, I was very tempted to take an "academic" approach to writing this book. After all, I've spent more than a decade being groomed for academia and learning the requisite "big words" for scholarship. But from the moment I wrote the first sentence, I knew that this would not be that type of book. *Believing Bigger* is a faith journey and I knew that I could not lead anyone down a road of faith unless I was willing to walk it myself. While I am not a private person, I tend to be a bit guarded because I have experienced firsthand how destructive people can be with personal information. So here was my test. I had to decide whether I would give others the power to judge me, as I have so many times before, or if I would rest in the peace of God's grace. Would I Believe Bigger than the mistakes I've made in the past, and share my life lessons in hopes of preventing others from experiencing the same hurt, headache, and heartbreaks?

In praying over this decision, I thought about the Samaritan Woman, better known as the Woman at the Well.[1] In most cases when people refer to the Samaritan Woman, they highlight her sin and linger on her sexual exploits. They never fail to mention the number of husbands she had, or the man that she was currently living with. They belabor the fact that she was a woman of ill reputation, and that she was likely the target of gossip and ridicule from the townspeople... that she voluntarily chose to risk personal injury and discomfort by filling her water pot when the sun would be at its highest, just to avoid the scorn of other women in the community. However, one of the most powerful shifts in her story is what happened after her encounter with Jesus. With great enthusiasm, she ran **boldly** to the very people she had been avoiding. She courageously approached the ones who had

---

[1] *See John 4:7-30*

shamed her and said, "Come, see a man who told me everything I ever did" (John 4:29).

That was her Believing Bigger moment. She faced her naysayers.She faced her accusers. She faced herself. Freed from the guilt and the shame of her past, she was liberated to tell others about Jesus because despite "everything she ever did," Jesus still extended love, kindness, and the gift of eternal life. For the same reasons, I am able to write this book. While I deeply regret a number of my choices in life, many rooted in a lack of faith, I am far more joyous that despite "everything I ever did," Jesus' love is greater than my faults. **He Believed Bigger in Me.** And because of that, I can share Him with you.

As you take this journey, my prayer is that you understand what it really means to Believe Bigger. For some of you, it will require you to Believe Bigger than your past. Others may have to Believe Bigger than a struggling marriage, a wayward child, a poor health diagnosis, an unfulfilled dream, the loss of a loved one, or lies from the devil himself. We all have something that keeps us from exercising the kind of faith that moves mountains, and I hope that even if you have to take it more than once, this journey will refresh your spirit, renew your mind and restore your faith.

One last thing… When your transformation begins, when you start to feel the shift from persecution to peace, from heartbroken to healed, and from broke down to breakthrough, I want you to *share your testimony.* Sometimes when we receive our deliverance from God, we forget that there are so many others who are still bound. *Believing Bigger* is to be shared. Take someone else on this journey. Start a faith circle with your friends or lead a class at your church. Create a special course during Vacation Bible School. Conduct a group counseling or mentoring session. There are many ways to help others Believe Bigger. I'm counting on you!

I also invite each of you to register for the Believing Bigger Faith Summit at www.believebiggersummit.com. There you will find additional downloads, registration info, and tips to lead others on this journey.

TALK TO ME

If you're on social media, let me know how this book is blessing you. You can find me on Twitter and Instagram, @ DrShanteSays, or on Facebook, fb.com/drshantesays. You can even email me, personally, at: testimony@believingbigger.com. When you reference the book on social media, use the hashtag #BelievingBigger31, and that will make it easier for me to find your comments, takeaways, and testimonies.

Ready?
Let's Start Believing Bigger!

1. WHO AM I?

"What is man that you are mindful of him,
and the son of man that you care for him?"
Psalms 8:4

"Mama's in the kitchen burning that rice...Daddy's on the corner just shooting that dice...Brother's in jail, raising Hell, Sister's on the corner selling fruit-cock-tail, Rockin' Robin..."

I didn't realize it at the time, but the words we sang as kids jumping rope had power. Our playtime soundtrack normalized things like poverty, broken homes, absent fathers, female promiscuity, and criminal behavior. Although too young to understand it, our childhood rhymes made these things acceptable and made us complicit in our own demise. We unwittingly set low expectations for ourselves and for our peers. At ages as young as 3 and 4 we would chant:

"Ooh! She think she cool...Cool enough to steal your dude.

Ooh! She think she fine... Fine enough to blow his mind.

Awww girl stop your lying! At least my (man) didn't leave me crying."

Just babies and we were already heralding the notion that we would compete for men and with one another, that we would use our bodies to keep a man happy, and that it was okay to bully and belittle our peers.

As an adult, it's sad to see how many of the things we sang about as children became reality and part of our identity. It is no wonder that so many of us struggle with insecurity and self-doubt. We keep replaying demoralizing lyrics in our heads, reminding us that we are destined to fail... subject to rejection... are made for a life of compromise. We're just not "good enough."

We were too young to realize it at the time, but we were under spiritual attack. The enemy attacks early and often, and young people are his favorite targets because they are so easy to influence. Those seemingly "innocent" songs from childhood were anything but. They were subtle, destructive, but effective seeds planted in our minds that have manifested in adulthood. Have you ever noticed how much easier it is to remember words when they are put to music? It's amazing what you can get people to say and do by adding a beat and a melody. Given Satan's musical background,[2] it's unsurprising that he has a cunning way of using music to get us to worship the very things God hates.

Over the course of your life, you may have encountered subtle and even obvious attacks that made you question your significance. This includes attacks on your identity, your confidence, your destiny, your marriage, your children, your friendships, your health, and your sanity. Satan's job is to steal, kill, and destroy,[3] so he knows that if he can create confusion, depression, fear or doubt, or haunt you with mistakes of the past, you will self-destruct. Even though no weapon formed against you will succeed,[4] if he can deter you long enough to make **you** do the dirty work for him, then his mission is complete.

Fortunately, God affirms our value and demonstrates it through His Word, and His love and favor upon us. So, the journey to Believing Bigger starts with knowing what God says about you and who He created you to be. The Bible says that God has crowned you with glory and honor.[5] A crown signifies majesty and royalty. You are a child of The King! Even King David was in awe of this description when he asked God in Psalms 8:4, "What is man that you are mindful of him?" David asked this question after he had reflected on the magnificence of God, the fact that God created the universe, the galaxies and everything within them, but still found value in David. He marveled that a God like that, could love

---

2 Ezekiel 28:12-15
3 John 10:10
4 Isaiah 54:7
5 Psalms 8:5

and care for us![6]

Regardless of what you may have spoken into your life before now, despite what anyone has said to you, or about you, it does not change what God has put in you, or who God says you are.

Scripture tells us that out of the same mouth we bless and we curse.[7] Start proclaiming blessings over your life. Bind the curses of "I'm broke," "I can't," "It's too late," and replace them with what God says about you and God's promises to you! Declare, "I'm rich in God's abundance towards me!" "I can do ALL things through Christ who gives me strength."[8] "I may be a late bloomer, but this is MY season!" Language creates reality. When God said, "I AM WHO I AM,"[9] that was His reassurance that He is everything we need Him to be. He is power. He is blessing. He is a healer. He is peace. And He created you in His image. God doesn't question your worthiness. Neither should you.

PRAY THIS

Lord, thank You for creating me in Your image. Thank You for loving me even when I don't always love myself. Bind every negative word ever spoken into my life and release every blessing that You have for me.

Give me the faith and the confidence to receive it.

Amen.

TWEET|POST THIS

I don't have to question who I am.
I know WHOSE I am and that's enough.
#BelievingBigger31

---

6 Psalms 8:9
7 James 3:10
8 John 3:16
9 Exodus 3:14

Believing Bigger: What messages do you need to silence in order to embrace your true identity in Christ?

"No one can make you feel inferior without your permission."
~ Eleanor Roosevelt

2. TAG! YOU'RE IT

"You did not choose me, but I chose you and appointed you so that you might go and bear fruit – fruit that will last – and so that whatever you ask in my name the Father will give you."
John 15:16

Many of us grew up with a daily regimen of outdoor activity: jumping rope, playing basketball, hide and seek, red light-green light, Simon Says, and many variations of Tag! In Tag, the slowest and heaviest kids became targets because they were easier to catch and less likely to tag the faster kids once they became "It". After awhile, these same kids stopped playing because they knew they were being exploited. They isolated themselves or sometimes just sat on the sidelines watching the other kids play.

Does this happen to you? Have you ever been chosen for a challenging assignment, not because you were valued, but because no one else wanted to be IT? Do you stop playing? Do you sit on the sidelines watching others succeed and excel while you remain stagnant and unengaged?

I recently partnered with an entrepreneur who crunches numbers by day, but whose true passion is preparing culinary masterpieces. I will never forget her reaction when I asked her to be the lead chef for one of my major events. Her eyes filled with tears when she spoke, "Thank you. You don't know how it feels to have someone finally see you and value you." She went on to share that while she trains people for supervisory positions at work, she remains in subordinate roles and frequently watches others get promoted and receive salary increases. She had gotten so used to being overlooked that she was overwhelmed when I chose her to take center stage at my event.

Thankfully, God sees all of your gifts because He is the one who gave them to you.[10] Those things you do exceptionally well – teaching, writing, creating, baking, coaching, taking photographs, whatever it is – are not accidents. They are gifts God specifically gave to you to impact the lives of other people. God is very clear that we did not choose Him; He chose us. While others may have overlooked you, God chose and equipped you with unique talents to serve the world. Unlike the childhood game, He tagged you **in spite** of your weaknesses, **not because** of them. In fact, God says that when we are weak, it gives Him an opportunity to be strong on our behalf.[11]

Too often we focus on what we can't do, don't have, or didn't get, instead of realizing that God is bigger, more powerful than any deficit. He has called us to a greater purpose, and will make up the difference for whatever we lack. He did it with Moses. He did it with David. He'll do it with you. When Moses led the children of Israel out of captivity, he didn't have a fraction of Pharaoh's army or his resources.[12] Moses had a staff, a tree branch to be exact. And When David fought Goliath, a 9 feet tall giant, God didn't furnish him with a white horse, a golden chariot, a blinged out machete, or a custom-made suit of armor.[13] David, a young boy, used what he had: a jerry-rigged slingshot and a handful of stones.

Though Moses and David faced seemingly insurmountable odds, and lacked the tools to give them a fighting chance, they did have FAITH. Moses declared victory before the sea was parted and assured the people that the Lord would make a way.[14] David declared victory before it was given to him so that everyone watching would know that God doesn't need "sword

---

10 Romans 12:3-8
11 2 Corinthians 12:9
12 Exodus 14:16-31
13 1 Samuel 17:40-50
14 Exodus 14:13

and spear" to fight the battle.[15] These two knew that it's not about what's in your hand, but whose hands you're in. They trusted God and believed that when He calls you, He will equip you. They understood God's promise that whatever you ask in Jesus' name to fulfill the mission that He has given you, He will provide.[16]

Just know that despite opposition, God has tagged you with a specific assignment, and whatever you need to accomplish that task, He will give to you.

PRAY THIS
Lord, I know that I have lacked courage to do the things You have called me to do because I looked at my limitations instead of Your limitless power. Forgive me, and equip me to go on the front lines to carry out Your will. In Jesus' Name. Amen.

TWEET|POST THIS
I may not have the best equipment, but I know the best Equipper.
I'm ready to Believe Bigger.
#BelievingBigger31

---

15 1 Samuel 17:47
16 John 14:13

Believing Bigger: What is God calling you to do that you feel ill-equipped, unprepared, or unqualified to achieve? How can being obedient to His call produce lasting fruit?

"I had to confront my fears and master my every demonic thought about inferiority, insecurity, or the fear of being black, young, and gifted in this Western culture."
~ Lauryn Hill

3. ANSWER THE CALL

"Then I heard the voice of the Lord saying, 'Whom shall I send? And who will go for us?' And I said, 'Here am I. Send me!'"
Isaiah 6:8

"Verdict: We the jury find George Zimmerman not guilty..."[17] These words sliced through my heart like a bad paper cut. Trayvon Martin, a teenage boy making a candy run, was just the latest victim of racial, social, and civil injustice. His life extinguished by a neighborhood vigilante who would now walk free. And across the country, there have been far too many more since him: Eric Garner in New York City, New York; Tamir Rice in Cleveland, Ohio; Michael Brown in Ferguson, Missouri; Sandra Bland in Waller County, Texas; LaQuan McDonald in Chicago, Illinois; the members of Emanuel AME Church in Charleston, South Carolina. With each one, my heart grew heavier and heavier! Solange Knowles captured the devastation of these events in a single Tweet:

Was already weary. Was already heavy hearted. Was already tired. Where can we be safe? Where can we be free? Where can we be black? ~Solange Knowles

In times of tragedy, most people try to make sense of what happened. But, there are never any easy answers. Typically, there is not a single person or group to blame for what occurred, and there are often many layers to the problem. Yet answers are what we look for. Like others, when I listened to the verdict in the Zimmerman case, I found myself looking for answers. Who was responsible for this child's death? Certainly Zimmerman was, but should others also be accountable? And how can we prevent such

---

17 Http://www.cnn.com/2013/07/13/justice/zimmerman-trial/

devastation from occurring in the first place? As these questions swirled through my mind, I could not help but think of what might have been prevented if someone had possessed the courage to answer the call. I am convinced that long before any of these tragedies occurred, many people – television show writers and producers, news journalists, parents, grandparents, teachers, other school personnel, coaches, officers, attorneys, judges – had opportunities to answer the call, the call to interrupt the cycle of typecasting, profiling, stereotyping, devaluing, ignoring, suspending, and incarcerating. But, somewhere, someone had failed to pick up.

Consider Barbara Henry. Most people have no idea who she is. They are better acquainted with her famous pupil, Ruby Bridges. Ruby is celebrated as the first black child to break the color barrier and attend a desegregated school in the South. She is applauded for her bravery and recognized as a champion for civil rights. But what many people don't know is that Barbara Henry was the only white teacher willing to teach Ruby. People don't know that parents pulled their children out of the school and out of Ruby's classroom making Ruby the ONLY student in Barbara Henry's class for an entire school year. Barbara was ostracized. Her life was threatened. She didn't have any friends. Her co-workers shunned her. And still, Barbara Henry answered the call.

Too many of us have not responded like Barbara Henry. For various reasons we have refused to answer the call.

We have allowed fear – fear of losing a job, losing friends, losing a man or woman, losing an election, losing money, losing status or power – to consume us. We doubt the power of our contributions. We ignore our responsibility. This is neither a justification nor a reprimand. It's just the truth. But, there are consequences when we don't answer the call.

Think, for a moment, about an eager radio listener calling a station to win concert tickets. Chances are that when she calls, she hears the incessant, annoying, and blaring sound of an unanswered phone that just keeps ringing… and ringing… and ringing… and ringing. Yet, the listener is persistent. She hangs up and redials in desperate hope that someone on the other end will answer and say that she is the right caller. She endures the nagging ring and busy signals until she tires and hangs up for good. In hanging up, she gives up hope of winning, all because no one answered the call.

Just like the radio station, someone is praying, begging, hoping that you will answer the call. But, how many of those people have called and never been answered? How many have hung up, called back, hoping this time, you will answer? How many have encountered your busy signal? And how many have hung for good believing that they don't have a chance? Someone is waiting for you to answer the call.

God is calling you out of your comfort zone. There are needs in this world yet to be met, and God is challenging you to use the gifts He's blessed you with to do more and reach more people. You are not destined for a life of clocking in and out of work, collecting a check, and going home. No! God wants to know, "Whom shall I send? And who will go for us?"[18] He is calling you to Believe Bigger than busywork. Answer the call.

Look at the Apostle Philip. He was busy doing God's work, saving souls, and having revival. He was putting points on the Kingdom Scoreboard. Yet, in the middle of the game, God called him out,[19] and sent him to the desert of all places. When he

18 Isaiah 6:8
19 See Acts 8:26-39

arrived, he found an Ethiopian reading the Book of Isaiah, and in need of someone to explain the Scripture to him. Because Philip answered the call, the Ethiopian man believed in Jesus as Savior and was baptized that day!

Like Philip, some of us are busy in the church, but God is calling us out into neighborhoods, cities and countries that need our help. Your faith journey is going to require you to lay aside excuses, fear, and some items on your "to-do" list. The Spirit of God is tugging at you. Yield to it. Your obedience can impact lives in ways that you cannot imagine. Answer the call.

PRAY THIS

Lord forgive me for being blinded by fear and distractions. Open my eyes so that I may see those who need my help. Give me the wisdom and the courage to answer the call. Amen.

TWEET|POST THIS

Someone is waiting for me to answer the call.
I'm picking up. Hello? I'm here.
#BelievingBigger31

Believing Bigger: What has been keeping you from answering the call? List any distractions that have kept you "too busy" to respond. Who might be waiting for you to show up?

"Inaction breeds doubt and fear. Action breeds confidence and courage. If you want to conquer fear, do not sit home and think about it. Go out and get busy."

~ Dale Carnegie

4. ON ONE CONDITION

> *"'If you can!' All things are possible for one who believes."*
> Mark 9:23

I have learned from experience that knowing something in your head is not the same as knowing it in your heart. If we're being completely honest, many of us pay lip service to faith in God. "Won't He Do It!" "Look at God!" "Won't He Will!" Yes, all of that sounds good, but our words belie our true convictions.

When I first started my business, I latched on to successful mentors, both real and virtual, to help keep me grounded and motivated. Their success inspired me...*initially*. And then, it intimidated me. I started "feeling some kind of way" when the things that seemed to happen for *them*, with relative ease, were not happening for me. I started comparing my chapter 1 to their chapter 21. I started inventing stories about why they were successful, while I was struggling to get started:

"They must have had the hook up."

"It's a Good Ole Boys Network."

"I'm sure it's politics; You gotta pay to play."

Despite attending church, every, single Sunday, I was plagued with doubt. Every week, I sang in the choir, went to Sunday school, and paid lip service to my faith in God. I had tons of head knowledge about God's power, but my heart failed me. While I believed God COULD bless my entrepreneurial endeavors, I just didn't know if He WOULD. It's amazing what we think God can and will do for **other** people, but not for us.

One Saturday, while delivering the keynote at a women's faith conference, I was overcome with conviction. I was being such a hypocrite. Here I was admonishing others to Believe Bigger than their doubts, while I went home plagued with my own. In that moment, I realized that *faith* is the key to our success or failure. When you have it, you unlock God's awesome power to move on your behalf. When you don't have it, you find yourself locked in a cage of fear, insecurity, doubt, disbelief, and depression.

Here's the thing about God – you can't hide anything from Him! Sure, you can post all of the right Facebook statuses… "(hashtag) #blessed," share a verse of the day on Instagram, and have others believing that you're a ride or die member of #TeamGod; but, God knows the truth. "These people come near me with their mouth and honor me with their lips, but their hearts are far from me."[20] God knows the desires of your heart. And He also knows whether you have faith that He will provide for you. The Bible references faith nearly 600 times. God knows that you are constantly subject to self-doubt and spiritual attack. That's why He reminds us, through His word, about His power to act on our behalf. But, in order to tap into God's power, we must satisfy **one condition…** and that is to have faith. Faith is a prerequisite to receiving all that God has for us.

Let me explain it this way, in Geometry, there is a principle called conditional logic. Conditional logic works on the **IF/THEN** principle. A conditional statement is considered TRUE if a logical connection is made between the hypothesis (p) and the conclusion (q). For example:

If I get eight hours of sleep (p), then I will be well rested in the morning (q). Notice the cause and effect nature of this statement: if I do **this***, then I get* **that***.*

Now look at God's conditional logic from Mark 9:23:

All thing are possible (q) for one who believes (p).

or

---

20 Isaiah 29:13

For one who believes (p), all things are possible (q).
If we accept this statement as
TRUE, then we must also accept that the opposite is true:
Nothing is possible (not q)
*for one who does not believe (not p).*or
If I do not believe (not p), then nothing will be possible (not q).
God's conditional logic proves that faith is the key that
unlocks the doors of restoration, reformation, influence, impact,
and success. And Jesus teaches us the power of our faith through
the narrative of a desperate father.

In the Gospel of Mark, Jesus encountered a hopeless father
whose son had been possessed by a spirit, which rendered him
deaf and mute. The father begged Jesus, "But if you can do
anything, have compassion on us and help us" (Mark 9:22). Jesus
repeated the father's words with indignation; "'**IF** you can?' **All**
things are possible for one who believes" (23, emphasis mine). At
that moment, the father shifted his focus from his son's physical
condition to his own spiritual condition, crying out,
"I believe; help my unbelief!" (24).

Perhaps you can relate to this father... desperate...
uncertain... seemingly out of options. You might also believe,
as he did, that what needs to change is *your situation,* when in
actuality, what may need to change is your **attitude** about your
situation. Intellectual knowledge of God is one thing, but sincere
faith is necessary for your heart to catch up to your mind.

When I envied the success of others, I was solely focused on
the *fruit* of their trees, rather than considering the root of their
trees. I had not once considered that the blessings they enjoyed
might have come from their unwavering faith. God doesn't

play favorites.[21] He doesn't have a bounty of blessings for some and table scraps for others. If you do your part, God will most assuredly do His.

PRAY THIS

Lord I want to believe that if I trust in You, You will direct my path. Help me to stop judging others when I don't know the whole story. Teach me to walk by faith and not by circumstance. Help my unbelief. Amen.

TWEET|POST THIS

I'm walking by faith, not by circumstance.
#BelievingBigger31

---

21 Romans 2:11

Believing Bigger: What story(ies) have you been telling yourself about why some things haven't turned out successfully? Where has your faith fallen short?

"There is nothing that wastes the body like worry, and one who has any faith in God should be ashamed to worry about anything whatsoever."
~ Mahatma Gandhi

5. ARE YOU MICROMANAGING GOD?

> *"But let him ask in faith, with no doubting, for the one who doubts is like a wave of the sea that is driven and tossed by the wind. For that person must not suppose that he will receive anything from the Lord."*
> James 1:6-7

In my early 20s, I was working as a program coordinator for a small, private college in the Midwest when the director of my department unexpectedly quit. Because our department was so small – only consisting of the director, an administrative assistant, another coordinator, and me – I automatically assumed that the other coordinator, who had been with the department for far longer than me, would succeed the outgoing director. As I expected, the other coordinator was named interim director and knew all of the logistics of the role. That's why I was surprised when the Dean asked me if I had planned to apply for the position. I had not. I hadn't even considered it. I had only been in the department for 11 months, but I figured the Dean was just trying to be fair by encouraging me to apply for the job.

After submitting my application, I really started thinking about the position – what worked well, what didn't, how to improve the office – and I decided to draft a strategic vision for the department. When I went to the interview, I distributed my strategic plan and walked the search committee through it. I was proud of myself for having taken the opportunity seriously, and for interviewing at that level, but I had zero expectation that I would get the job. The other candidate was 15 years my senior, had more experience, and was already in the interim role. Apparently, none of that mattered to the committee. They were so impressed with my presentation that despite my lack of experience, they believed in my vision.

I was the unanimous choice.

When the committee announced that I would be the new director… All. Hell. Broke. Loose. The other candidate lodged bogus complaints against me, saying that I had been coached before my interview and that I had been given the interview questions ahead of time. And because I am black, she even claimed reverse discrimination was the culprit for her failure to receive the position.

My interim supervisor turned direct report then dropped a pile of work on my desk and told me that, *effective immediately,* she would no longer handle any interim duties, that I should not expect her to train me because a director should "know how to run her department," that she would not be coming in early or staying late, and that this was not personal, just business. To say that it was a hostile environment would be putting it mildly. From the day I took office, she started keeping a "file" on me. She printed every email I sent and kept a paper trail in hopes of finding something useful to prove my "incompetence." She questioned every decision I made and kept close tabs on me the entire first year of my job as director. Although I was her supervisor, **she** was micromanaging **me.**

Has this ever happened to you? Have you ever had to deal with someone constantly undermining your authority? Criticizing your every move? Waiting for evidence that you are incapable of being in charge? Well, that is **exactly** what we do to God when we pray for something and start having doubts about whether He will answer.

James 1:7-8 warns about being "double-minded," and tells us that if we ask anything of God, we should do so without doubting. Many times we petition God in prayer only to turn around and micromanage Him at every step. But, how many times has God proven His faithfulness, trustworthiness, and ability to deliver in times of need? Yet we still do not trust His leadership. We get *impatient*. We get *indignant*. And then we get in motion doing things the way WE think they ought to be done. James says that a person like this should not expect to receive ANYTHING from the Lord.[22]

This faith journey requires a shift in your mindset. First, you must acknowledge that your scope of vision and understanding is limited. Second, you must accept that God, who sees the past, present, and the future, knows how to answer your prayer in a way that will give HIM glory and you peace. And third, you must trust that He will answer, not how and when you want, but in the time and manner best for you. Amen? Amen!

PRAY THIS

Lord, thank you for loving me, being patient with me, and forgiving me, especially when I try to do YOUR job. I know that You are more than capable. Help me to stop being anxious and trust that You will act on Your schedule, not mine. Amen.

TWEET|POST THIS

When it comes to running my life, God is the best candidate for the job. #BelievingBigger31

---

22 James 1:8

Believing Bigger: In what ways have you micromanaged God? What do you need to trust Him for right now?

"The manager accepts the status quo; the leader challenges it."
~ Warren Bennis

6. DADDY ISSUES

"Though my father and mother forsake me, the Lord will receive me."
Psalms 27:10

"Oh I'm 1000% SURE he's the father!" Shimeka insisted.

I don't watch the show, but the paternity episodes on Maury have become a pop culture sensation. I recently saw a clip on YouTube where Maury mediated an argument between Shimeka, her mother, and Bobby, the alleged father of Shimeka's young son. When Maury finally opened the famous envelope disclosing the paternity results, the three of them stopped bickering and set their gaze on the piece of paper.

*"Bobby... you are **NOT** the father!"*

Shimeka quickly exited the stage. Her mother shook her head in disbelief, while Bobby reacted with sheer exuberance. He leapt from his chair and victory danced his way all over the set, high-fiving audience members like he had just won the lottery, as rap music blasted in the background. Meanwhile, Shimeka's son, woefully unaware of his exploitation, looked on from the green room, clueless about what had just happened.

This short clip was a sad and shameful display underscoring a painful legacy of absent fathers and neglected children in America. What we see in our country today is a drastic departure from God's plan for marriage and family.[23] God gave fathers the responsibility of protector, provider, and priest. But today many fathers have inconsistent or even nonexistent roles in their children's lives, and the impact of their absence is widely felt. The Department of Correction in Fulton County, Georgia reports that 85% of youth in prisons come from fatherless homes.

---

23 Genesis 2:18-25

And this is just one example.

I can personally attribute the vast majority of my biggest mistakes to the insecurity I had growing up without a father. In my mind, a man was the guaranteed path to security. Having a man around would ensure that the family had a double income, lower household costs, and overall financial independence. He would keep the family safe and love unconditionally. The man was the figurehead for my "picture perfect" family, so I spent much of my life searching for one who would bring me the security I never knew as a child. I did not realize that I had been Looking for Love in all the Wrong Places. I did not realize that love, happiness, security, peace and joy are wrapped up in God. In fact, it was very difficult for me to trust God when I was young.

I already had ONE invisible father.

How was I supposed to depend on ANOTHER?

But, I thank God for His faithfulness toward me and the promises of His Word. You see, absentee fathers are nothing new to God.[24] He knew that some men would not accept their positions as fathers, but He promised to stand in the gap and make up the difference. Before God sent a loving stepfather into my life, I marveled at how my mother, who was making a fraction of what I make now, was able to raise two children on her own, without child support or alimony. It wasn't easy. But God made a way. God kept His promise to her. And God kept his promise concerning me. Once I realized that God was the only one who could secure my future, I found peace.

Thankfully, our Heavenly Father is nothing like the men who abandon their children. He promises to never leave us or

---

24 Psalms 68:5

abandon us,[25] even during our darkest moments.[26] He commits to lifting us up when our earthly parents fall short.[27] And He assures us that we will never be without our basic necessities.[28] God knows what we need before we ask,[29] and has made provision for us to be with Him once we transition from earth to Heaven.[30] Now that's a protector, provider, and priest!

If you're like me, you too may have struggled with Daddy issues. But, I challenge you to stop chasing people and things for security, and to chase after God. God wants you to seek Him. He wants you to trust Him. He wants you to turn to Him first.[31] God is not adverse to you being financially stable, happily married, or fulfilled in your job.[32] He just wants you to know that HE IS THE SOURCE of those things.

PRAY THIS

Lord, thank You for being my first father. Thank You for making provision for me even when I thought I needed more. Thank You for filling the gap, making a way, and staying true to Your word. Thank You for owning me as Your child. Amen.

TWEET|POST THIS

The paternity results are in; "God is the Father!"
#BelievingBigger31

---

25 Deuteronomy 31:6; Matthew 28:20
26 Psalms 23:4
27 Psalms 27:10
28 Psalms 37:25
29 Matthew 6:8
30 John 14:2-3
31 Matthew 6:33
32 Psalms 84:11

Believing Bigger: Have you ever experienced earthly or spiritual daddy issues? How has God shown His ability to be a father to you?

"It is easier for a father to have children than for children to have a real father."

~ Pope John XXIII

7. HATERS GONNA HATE

> *"As the ark of the Lord was entering the City of David, Michal daughter of Saul watched from a window. And when she saw King David leaping and dancing before the Lord, she despised him in her heart." 2 Samuel 6:16*

In the Disney movie, The Lion King, after learning that he would become the next king of Pride Rock, a young Simba excitedly ran to share the news with his uncle Scar. Scar, bitter and full of envy, managed a dry, "I'm happy for you." The future that Simba described was the very one that Scar coveted for himself. Despite their family ties, Scar could not move beyond his own selfish motives to feel genuine happiness for his nephew. Instead, narcissism corrupted his thinking and led him into an evil plot. Scar proved, like Rev. Kenneth E. Copeland once preached, that "everybody that's in your **circle** ain't necessarily in your **corner.**"

Like Simba's kingship, the calling God intends for your life is often a purpose far exceeding anything you ever imagined. God's plan for you is bigger, more amazing than even a young cub dreaming about becoming king. But, while God has a plan for your life, like Scar, other people have plans for you too. These plans, frequently from family members, are usually expressed by passive expectations or direct demands. I have worked with many clients who are frustrated, hurt, even depressed by the lack of support they have received from family and loved ones. These same clients had gone out of their way to be there and provide support for others, but when they began to pursue their God-given passions, were questioned, criticized, and doubted.

"You're doing what?"

"Seriously?"

"At Your Age? Who Does That?!"

King David experienced similar resistance from his own wife. When he brought the Ark of the Lord to Jerusalem, David was so excited that he began to dance.[33] His dance was one of sheer jubilation because the Ark of the Lord represented the presence of God, His holiness and faithfulness to the people of Israel. So, David's dance was a moment of ecstatic praise. Nowadays, we would say he "caught the Holy Ghost."

As the King danced, his wife Michal watched from the window. She thought David looked like a fool and found it was distasteful for a king to act so "common." While the kingdom celebrated with David, Michal secretly despised him in her heart. David did not meet her expectations of what a king should be and his actions did not coincide with her understanding of what a king should do. Michal had drank a tall glass of haterade.

By the time King David came in to bless his household, his wife was waiting for him *"at the doe!"* She mocked him, told him that he humiliated himself in front of the peasants like a common thug. But David stood firm. He made it clear that he danced before the Lord as a symbol of worship and reverence, and that he would do it again in a minute. He told her that the peasants she spoke of, actually held him in high regard. David was more respected outside of his home than he was by his own wife, but he was secure in his praise.

Just like King David, everyone will not understand your praise. And that's okay. God knows how to handle them. You see, hating on the successes of others has a price tag. In Michal's case, God closed her womb; she became barren and did not have any children. This is significant because, in biblical times, it was a great honor to be a first wife, especially when that wife bore the

---

33 *See 2 Samuel 6:16-23*

first son. Any male children Michal would have had would have been first in line for the kingdom. However, when she despised David's praise, she destroyed any chance of carrying on her lineage. Her scorn for David resulted in a significant loss.

Let's be honest, sometimes we are the hated and sometimes times we are the hater. There are times when seeing someone else's blessing makes us long for the things we want for ourselves. Before we know it, we start "feeling some kind of way." And this is a dangerous place to be. It is a prime position for the enemy to get into your head. The enemy would have you believe that God plays favorites, that others are worthy, but you are not. Don't fall for it. God is not a respecter of persons.[34] We've all done enough dirt to be disqualified from His blessings. So, don't block your breakthrough by coveting someone else's. Even if you never express it outwardly, God knows what it is in your heart. If you have been guilty of this, pray; ask God's forgiveness.

If you have been a victim of it, still pray.
Pray that you do not become emotionally wounded and pray for those who are persecuting you.[35]
The enemy's job is to make you doubt God's calling over your life and he will use any means necessary, even those closest to you, to instill fear, guilt, or insecurity. During your faith journey, you will undoubtedly be forced to reckon with haters. They key is remembering that whom God blesses, no man can curse![36]

---

34 Acts 10:34-35
35 Matthew 5:44; Luke 6:27-28
36 Number 23:8

PRAY THIS

Lord, nothing is hidden from You, not even the things in my heart. Reveal any feelings of jealousy or envy towards others and remove them. Protect me from the emotional daggers of the enemy as You elevate me to do Your work. Amen.

TWEET|POST THIS

God can humble and handle my haters. Blessed and Unbothered. #BelievingBigger31

Believing Bigger: In what ways have you been made to feel guilty or insecure about pursuing your calling? What would you be able to do if you were not fearful or insecure about the opinions of others?

"You will face your greatest opposition when you are closest to your biggest miracle."

~ Shannon Alder

8. SCARCITY

> *"You did not choose me, but I chose you and appointed you*
> *so that you might go and bear fruit – fruit that will last – and so*
> *that whatever you ask in my name the Father will give you."*
> John 15:16

I'm not an accountant, but I have a basic grasp on the principles of finance. For example, if you have $100 in your checking account and you withdraw $20, you will have $80 remaining. Simple. Basic. Logical. Simple math is necessary for economic survival, while God's equation for abundance is necessary for spiritual survival. God's methods of calculation are vastly different than ours. When we give, we give out of our existing resources. So, the more we give, the less we have. When God gives, He gives according to His endless supply. In essence, the more He gives, the more He has available to give because God is not a resource, He is the source.

Because of the basic financial principles I described above, many people find it difficult to give. Think about the number of people who are one paycheck away from poverty or a life changing circumstance. You may be one of them. Unfortunately, Americans lag behind 34 developed countries when it comes to having money in savings, with the typical household averaging less than 5% of their annual income. This results in the constant fear of running out, not having enough, or being unable to maintain a particular standard of living. But scarcity isn't just a lack of physical resources; scarcity is also a mindset.

Consider the vast world of entrepreneurship. I've heard countless stories of successful entrepreneurs who were less than forthcoming about their formula for success. Many believe, "if I share it, others will use it; and if others use it, they will create a shortage for me." As a result, these brilliant minds tend to give vague answers to inquiries about their business acumen, seldom respond to requests for meetings, and keep their inner circle tight and exclusive. What they don't realize is that despite any financial wealth their business has acquired, they are still broke. Poverty and scarcity reside in their minds because they fail to understand that if God can bless you once, He can do it again… and again… and again.

When we hoard or withhold our blessings from others, we demonstrate a lack of faith in God. When we are unwilling to share our gifts and talents, we close the door to future blessings. We may not say it with our mouths, but our actions expose our lack of conviction. Our actions reveal those secret thoughts that good things happened because we "got lucky," "were in the right place at the right time," or as my Granny used to say, "hit a lick." But, we must discard these thoughts and understand that "every good and perfect gift is from above."[37]

Know that what God has for you is for you. You don't have to live in fear of losing what you have because God promised to supply all of your needs according to His riches.[38] And God's supply of blessings is everlasting. It's never ending. It's pressed down, shaken together, and running over. Think about it this way, when the trashcan gets full and people are too lazy to take it out, they will **press it down** to make room for more deposits. Once the contents can no longer be pressed down, the can will start **running over.** This is how God's equation of abundance works. When you give abundantly and generously to others, God promises that it will be given back to you with *interest*. He will fill up your "can" until it overflows. This truth can be very difficult to grasp because we keep trying to apply simple math to our

---

37 James 1:17
38 Philippians 4:19

all-powerful God. When we apply earthly principles to spiritual matters, it just doesn't add up. But God's ways are not our ways and His thoughts are not our thoughts.[39]

Your faith journey is going to require you to set aside your way for God's way. Give freely and it will be given back to you. But, let me stop here and caution you. You should never give just to get. It is very easy to get trapped doing the right thing for the wrong reasons or with the wrong motives.[40] So, it is important to remember that giving is an expression of love, for God and for those that God wants you to bless. When you understand this, your "payout" for giving your time, your talents, and your treasures to help others will be returned to you in ways that exceed your bank account. You will be prosperous in ways that cannot be counted in dollars and cents – good health, peace of mind, family protection, loyal friendships, genuine joy. So don't stand in the corner trying to protect crumbs. Step out, by faith, and start giving to the people you were called to serve.

PRAY THIS

Lord thank You for giving so generously, especially when we don't deserve it. Allow me to give and to serve with the right spirit, without fear and without looking for recognition. Amen.

TWEET|POST THIS

Broke people give to get. Rich people get to give.
#BelievingBigger31

---

39 Isaiah 55:8
40 Matthew 6:1-4

Believing Bigger: Besides money, how do you define success? How can your success benefit others?

"Remember that the happiest people are not those getting more, but those giving more."

~ H. Jackson Brown, Jr

9. AMERICAN IDOL

> "'You fool! This very night your life will be demanded from you. Then who will get what you have prepared for yourself?' This is how it will be with whoever stores up things for themselves but is not rich toward God."
> Luke 12:20-21

At first glance, you might think that God has something against rich people. There are more than 170 Bible verses on money, 60 of which warn against greed specifically. However, God does not take issue with any of us being wealthy. He takes issue when the pursuit of riches takes priority over our commitment to Him. God is not shy about wanting first place in our lives and makes it quite clear that He's the jealous type.[41] As the young folks say, God is not "the one" to be "treated".

In the parable of the rich fool, Jesus tells the story of a man who had acquired great wealth. He had become so affluent that he did not have room to store his extra harvest. So he decided to destroy his existing storehouse to build bigger, better, new and improved facilities. His plan, then, was to kick back, relax, sip Mai-Tais, and live like a BOSS!

There was just one problem; **he died that night.**

Let that sink in for a minute. Think about how hard you work on your job...overtime, bonus projects to bring in extra money, a side-hustle here and there. And for what? The good life? This parable illustrates that no matter how many jobs you have, how much money you bring in, or how good your credit score is, God is ultimately in control of what happens next. Money and wealth do not guarantee a good life, or a long and prosperous one. Only God can give and sustain life.[42] But, the rich fool was so busy building his empire that he had neglected to build his relationship

---

41 Deuteronomy 4:24
42 Psalms 54:4

with God. How did the Lord respond? You fool! This very night your life will be demanded from you. Then who will get what you have prepared for yourself?" (20).

Are you like this man? Are you so busy making a living that you've neglected to make a life...one that includes giving God priority? The rich fool didn't just receive a death sentence. He was also met with the shocking realization that every, single thing he had worked and slaved for, **somebody else** would enjoy, and there was nothing – not one thing – he could do about it. But, how do you think God would have responded if the rich man had said, *"Lord, thank You, for this abundant blessing. I have much more than I could want or need; accept my offering and please show me who I can bless with extra goods and extra jobs so that men and women can support their families."*

During your faith journey, you may be tempted to revel in your own success and forget who brought such blessings to you. But, you must avoid that trap. The more successful you are, the more people will want from you and the greater the demand on your time and your resources. It can become very easy to shift your attention from God to your growing success. You wake up in the morning and reach for your cell phone instead of your Bible. Before you've wiped the crust out of your eyes, you're reviewing your calendar, checking emails, and updating social media statuses. The time you once had for prayer and meditation has been replaced by work and other distractions. You start missing church...first one service, then another. Before you know it, you've missed a month of Sundays. The devil will use anything, including your success, to distract you from your commitment to God. How do I know? I was guilty of the same thing! I was guilty of idolatry. Idolatry is anything or anyone that takes God's place, and can look as innocent as this:

Can't make it to church, Junior has a football game...
Oh, see I would have gone on that mission trip, but it was the same
date as our annual golf outing...
I would come to Bible study, but I get off work too late...

It may be your job, your kids, your cell phone, your boo thang, or your Saturday night shenanigans, but many of us have eased God out of 1st place. I can tell you from experience, though, that once you start pushing God to the back burner, He will most certainly get your attention. He will allow things to happen in your life that will not so subtly remind you just how much you need Him. Don't believe me? Read the Old Testament. The children of Israel were the original BeBe's Kids.[43] Each time they abandoned God and His ways, they went into bondage.[44]

God doesn't want you to be broke. He just wants to make sure that your devotion is to the Provider instead of the provision. He promises that if you seek Him first, He will bless the rest.[45]

PRAY THIS

Lord, You have never put me on the back burner. Help me to realign my priorities so that You remain first in my life. Remove every excuse, scheduling conflict, and idol that distracts me from building my relationship with You. Amen.

TWEET|POST THIS

Let me be sure to update my spiritual status
before I update my social status.
#BelievingBigger31

---

43 Original characters created by comedian, Robin Harris.
44 Jeremiah 1:16
45 Matthew 6:33

Believing Bigger: Have you ever placed God on the back burner? How did He respond? In what ways can you give God priority during your pursuit of success?

"Idolatry is really not good for anyone. Not even the idols."
~ John Bach

10. ONE OF THESE KIDS IS DOING HIS OWN THING

> *"But you are a chosen people, a royal priesthood, a holy nation, God's special possession, that you may declare the praises of him who called you out of darkness into his wonderful light."*
> *1 Peter 2:9*

"Three of these kids belong together... three of these kids are kind of the same... one of these kids is doing his own thing, now it's time to play our game..." In the 70's, this song was all the rage on Sesame Street. Routinely, characters on the show would put a group of similar objects or people together and include an object or person that didn't match the others. The goal was to see if children could identify the object or person that stood out from the rest. Nowadays, it can be hard to distinguish those who have a relationship with God from those who don't. People know more about the Lyon's Den on Empire than they do about the Lion's Den where God blessed Daniel for taking a bold stand.[46] Christians look too much like the world.

I often notice this when I ask people to define success. Many explain their version of success by talking about the kind of house they want to live in, how much money they want in the bank, how many weeks of vacation they'd like to have, the kind of car they want to drive and, among other things, what colleges they want their kids to go to. When I probe and ask, **how** these things make them successful, it gets so quiet you can hear an ant crawling on a cotton ball. The truth is, they don't know. That's because society has brainwashed us into believing that success is equal to material wealth and power. By these metrics, we think being the envy of our peers, having what others struggle to attain, and flaunting our possessions is a win. Kanye West put it this way, *"And I spent 400*

---

46 Daniel 6:1-28

bucks on this, just to be like n---a, you ain't up on this!"

But, this is a reckless and dangerous way to make decisions. Trying to one up someone is futile, as is chasing money just to buy more stuff. Even when we see others living what looks like the dream, what those individuals project is usually an incomplete story of their "success." For example, there are well documented stories of young men lured into drug dealing and gang activity based on a glamorized lifestyle of quick money, fast cars, and loose women. What they fail to notice is that the luxury car is leased, not owned; the only people making money are the top dogs, not the low-level dope boys; and that loose women are scarce for those at the bottom of the totem pole. These misguided youngsters glorify the lifestyle, but never count the costs. This is exactly the temptation Jesus warned against when he said, "For wide is the gate and broad is the road that leads to destruction, and many enter through it."47 Bright lights, big city, fame and fortune sound good, but all that glitters is not gold. The problem is that sometimes we struggle with a sense of entitlement. "I work hard, so I deserve…" Millions of Americans are currently drowning in debt trying to finance a lifestyle that mirrors something or someone they saw on TV. A well-known quote, often misattributed to actor Will Smith, puts it this way:

Too many people are buying things they don't need
With money they don't have,
To impress people they don't even like.

Your faith journey will require you expand your definition of success.

I grew up in a household where we didn't have very many material things. But, in hindsight, I realize I was spoiled. I never

---

47 Matthew 7:13

wanted for food or shelter, and my family always looked out for me. Yet when my peers were rocking the latest pair of Jordans, Air Force Ones, Girbaud Jeans, or brand new Starter Jackets, none of that mattered. While they flaunted high priced threads, I was still waiting to get my clothes off layaway! It always bothered me that I couldn't have what they had when they had it because I did not understand the value of money or hard work. I did not understand that those things did not truly define success. Because of this, I graduated from college with six credit cards and a job making $12/hour.

While it is human nature to desire the latest trends, some of us move beyond desire and secretly covet others' possessions, their businesses, relationships, social circles, and popularity. We get caught up in the material hype. But God has called us to stand out from the crowd. He says that we are "peculiar" and "set apart" for His glory and His use. God's will for your life may not always be trendy, but the rewards of obedience far outweigh the sacrifices of disobedience. Are you ready to be the kid that's doing his own thing?

PRAY THIS

Lord, I believe that You will not withhold anything that You want me to have. Fix my gaze on the blessings of my life, and not take them for granted. Release any impulse to keep up with the Joneses and increase my desire to keep up with Jesus. Amen.

TWEET|POST THIS

Everything that I need, I have. Grateful.
#BelievingBigger31

Believing Bigger: Reflect on a time where you jumped on the bandwagon or envied someone else's success. What was at the root of your feelings/actions? What were you really seeking? Approval? Acceptance? Acknowledgment?

"Your time is limited; so don't waste it living someone else's life."
~ Steve Jobs

11. CLAP BACK SEASON

> *"As for you, you meant evil against me, but God meant it for good..." Genesis 50:20a*

Believe it or not, some people in your life don't want you to succeed. They may never say it out loud, but you know it by their actions. You hear it in their slick comments. And you sense the negative vibes when you talk about your accomplishments. This is because, in many ways, success functions like a mirror, revealing what the other person has or has not accomplished in their own lives. How people react to their reflection in this mirror varies greatly. Some react favorably, using another person's progress as motivation and inspiration. Some are indifferent, hitting you with the nonchalant, "good for you." But many more, when they see you winning, feel threatened, insecure, envious, or jealous. Sadly, those who fall in the last category are often the people closest to you – your spouse, other family, good friends, church members, or co-workers. What is surprising, though, is that this type of jealously has been occurring since the beginning of time.

In Genesis 37, we meet Jacob's son, Joseph.[48] God had given Joseph the gift of dream interpretation and placed a special calling on Joseph's life that even his father must have sensed because he favored Joseph among all of his brothers. And the brothers despised Joseph because of it. They did not see what their father saw. They did not understand what made Joseph so special. And they were jealous of him. So, Joseph's brothers conspired to kill him and then lied about it.

You may not have endured a plot to take your life, but I'm sure many of you have dealt with tension from friends and family because of a special relationship or a unique talent you had.

---

[48] See Genesis 37-50 for a full account of Joseph's story

Maybe you're still dealing with a jealous spouse, a critical mother, insecure siblings, a resentful child, or a now-distant friend. Their attitudes do not physically harm you, but emotionally and spiritually, you are broken. You may even have slowed your progress because of these naysayers, but Believing Bigger challenges you to trust God and stop limiting your opportunities to make others comfortable. Either they will catch up or fall off. Now that may sound harsh and it's not always easy to accept, but too many people hate when you're experiencing success, but love it when you struggle. Notice how many friends you have when things in your life are falling apart? That's because misery loves company. Just like the success mirror, misery also reflects what is or isn't going right in the other person's life. Those who feed on negativity feign support when you're down because they can relate more to what's wrong in your life than to what is going right. In fact, they don't mind when you lean on them because it reminds them that they are not alone. But when your situation improves, they disappear. But you have to understand that whether these persons applaud you or curse you, love you or leave you, God remains and empowers you for success.

Look again at Joseph. Despite his brothers' plan to kill him, God protected Joseph. Though they sold him into slavery, God kept Joseph from harm. Though he endured many trials – prison, abandonment, false accusations, and betrayal – God set Joseph up for the ultimate clap back.49 God's favor was always upon him. In the midst of his enslavement, Joseph became second in command in Egypt. His brothers were humbled before him; they were forced to admit their betrayal and begged for their lives.

---

49 A clap back is a targeted comeback designed to shut down, once and for all, any person who thinks it is okay to attack you, leaving them humiliated, dumbfounded, and shamed.

With one word, Joseph could have fed his brothers to the dogs. But Joseph had vision. He saw the bigger picture and understood that his setbacks were stepping-stones for his comeback.

When it seemed like Joseph's brothers had triumphed over him, Joseph knew that what they meant for evil, God meant for good (Genesis 50:20).

This faith journey requires you to have vision like Joseph. When things fall apart, as they most certainly will sometimes, or when people you thought supported you turn their backs on you, trust that there is a bigger purpose. Know that the enemy is especially fond of attacking family, or "family-like," relationships because those are the ones likely to hurt us the most. But what the enemy means for evil, God can use for our good.50 We only see a fragment of the picture, but God sees the entire landscape. Trust Him with your life!

Joseph did not have any easy road, but he trusted God every step of the way, and God sustained him through the hardships. Joseph's brothers did not recognize his value, but God did. And that is all that matters. Too often we seek approval and validation in the wrong places. But if God is for us, then who can be against us?51

So when it seems like the enemy is winning or that your detractors will have the last laugh, keep it moving. God knows what He has invested in you; and He knows what experiences will yield the best return. Don't waste your energy plotting revenge, being petty, throwing subtle jabs, or posting Facebook blasts. God invented the clap back; pray and let Him handle it.52

---

50 Romans 8:28
51 Romans 8:31
52 Psalm 105:12-15, Romans 12:19

PRAY THIS

Lord, You said to "count it all joy" when we fall into various trials because the trying of our faith produces patience. Help me to be patient through trials knowing that You are preparing me for greater things to come. Release me from bitterness and protect me from those who seek to sabotage my success. Amen.

TWEET|POST THIS

God's approval means the enemy's removal.
#BelievingBigger31

Believing Bigger: Can you recall a time where it seemed like things were falling apart, but later realized they were actually coming together? What happened? How did God show His faithfulness during this season?

"The best revenge is massive success."
~ *Frank Sinatra*

12. DOWN, BUT NOT OUT

"No one from the east or the west or from the desert can exalt themselves. It is God who judges: He brings one down, and exalts another."
Psalm 75:6-7

In November 2007, I was a single mom, with a very active and very talkative one year-old. And, I was a doctoral student. Though I had completed my classes, I still had that pesky research paper (dissertation) looming over my head. The previous year, I had spent a good chunk of my maternity leave writing a 30-page exam that had to be completed before I could even begin writing the actual dissertation. I was a nursing mom, so pumping time became writing time. It was not uncommon to see me pumping, typing, and rocking the baby to sleep with my foot on her bassinette. The whole experience left me exhausted and less than eager to finish my degree. I kept putting off the dissertation until opportunity came knocking.

After teaching for years as a part-time adjunct, my ultimate goal was a full time professorship. So when I learned, in the fall of 2007, that a local college had not one, but FOUR, full-time, tenure track positions open in my discipline, I thought, "Hallelujah! This is the chance I've been waiting for." One of my co-workers, who was working on a similar degree, also heard about the openings and we agreed to keep each other in the loop regarding the hiring process. Weeks after I had submitted my application, I still hadn't heard a peep from the college. It also occurred to me that I had not heard anything from my colleague either. When I asked her if she had any news, I was surprised to find out that she already had a phone interview, but had not moved forward in the process.

My mind started racing:

"Phone interview? We applied at the same time. Why haven't I

heard anything?"

"Phone interview? Why didn't she say anything before now?"

"Phone interview? Why would they call her and not me? We work at the same place. In fact, I'm a director, and she's a coordinator."

"Maybe she has more experience?"

"Maybe she's further along in her degree?"

"Maybe this is my fault? If only I didn't procrastinate on finishing my research paper."

"Wait...! If they're on phone interviews, doesn't that mean that the search process is in full swing?"

A few days later, I finally did hear from the college. It was a simple letter. I was rejected. *"Thank you for applying... we appreciate your interest... you have not moved forward... we wish you well on your search..."* I was hurt. I was more than hurt. I was angry-hurt. Being an adjunct professor meant I was working two jobs to support the baby, pay the mortgage, and all of my other bills. I spent my days working a full time job and my nights teaching, two and sometimes three classes at a time. A full professorship meant higher income, flexible scheduling, and better benefits. And more flexibility in my schedule meant I could spend more time with my daughter. I needed this! I wanted it sooooo badly that I had been romanticizing about how awesome life would be when I got it. And I felt actual pain when it slipped out of my grasp! It hurt. I was devastated.

So I did the only thing I could do. I prayed. I didn't pray that God would reverse the decision. I prayed that He give me the peace and faith to accept His will, and God answered. During my prayer, I heard God's voice. He said, "I got you." I immediately felt peace. Weeks later, I received a phone call from the college. Someone had been investigating the hiring practices and my application raised a red flag. Based on the investigator's assessment, I should have at least gotten a phone interview because my application clearly met, and in some areas exceeded, the minimum qualifications of the position. Within two weeks of that call, my application had gone from the reject pile to the top of the list. And by May 2008, after three rounds of interviews, I was offered a position! But there was a catch... Without a completed and successfully defended dissertation, I would be hired at an instructor level, making the same salary I made at my current job. However, if I completed the dissertation by the time the school year began in August, I would be hired as an assistant professor and make $12K more than my current job. "No problem!" I told them. Except there was a problem, a very BIG one! I only had three months to write, edit, and defend a paper that takes some people years, but certainly longer than a few months to write. I panicked! Even though God had just worked a miracle in my favor, I lost my enthusiasm because the opportunity again felt unattainable. But, I remembered Matthew 19:26, "Jesus looked at them and said, 'With man this is impossible, but with God all things are possible.'" I told myself that I had originally been overlooked because I had not finished my doctoral degree, but God had made a way for me anyway. I was determined to finish what I started, even if it looked like an insurmountable task.

Over the next six weeks, I worked my full time job, took care of my baby, put her to bed, researched and wrote from 9:00 p.m. to 3:00 a.m. Every day. Every night. Every weekend. Without fail, I wrote, and wrote, and I wrote. By the grace of God, I finished my dissertation on July 4, 2008 and successfully defended it two weeks later! God had made the impossible possible! The icing on the cake, though, is that not only did I complete my dissertation so I could enter this new job as a full time, tenure track professor, but I ended up being the only one in the department with a doctorate.

This meant that I started, on day 1, as the highest ranked and highest paid member of the department! And eight years later, this is still true!

When things don't work out as you planned, remember that they will always work out as God plans. A rejection from man cannot stand against an approval from God. When God says, "I got you," He means it. When you operate under the power of His Spirit, anything is possible, even a year-long research paper can manifest in 6 weeks. So listen for His voice, and trust Him. He fixed my situation in such a way that I could not help but to give Him the credit, and He can do the same for you. Your faith journey will be full of disappointments, but God promises that in His timing, we will reap a harvest if we do not give up.[53]

PRAY THIS

Lord help me to keep disappointment from turning into self-doubt. I know that what You have for me is assigned to me specifically and that Your plans for my life are far greater than my own. Give me the confidence to believe You when You speak blessings into my life. Amen.

TWEET|POST THIS

When God Says Yes, Nobody Can Say No
#BelievingBigger31

---

53 Galatians 6:9

Believing Bigger: Have you ever let someone else's rejection cause you to doubt yourself? Why is it so easy to accept someone else's opinion as gospel instead of the actual gospel?

"A rejection is nothing more than a necessary step in the pursuit of success."

~ Bo Bennett

13. UNFAITHFUL

> *"His master replied, 'Well done, good and faithful servant!*
> *You have been faithful with a few things; I will put you in charge*
> *of many things. Come and share your master's happiness!'"*
> Matthew 25:21, 23

When most people hear the word "unfaithful," they immediately think of a romantic relationship gone wrong. But being unfaithful has broader implications than sexual infidelity. To be unfaithful means straying from one's commitment, allegiance, or duty. It means to be reckless and irresponsible; to mishandle or neglect. And this covers all aspects of life, not just relationships. It even covers how we handle money.

Now, I'd love to say that I have a perfect credit score, but I don't. And I'd love to say that I started building my nest egg in my early 20s, but I didn't. And I'd even love to say that I have always paid my bills on time, but I haven't. The truth is, two months before my 18th birthday, I applied for and received my first credit card. Being 17 years-old with a minimum wage job, and now a credit card, was a recipe for disaster. I suddenly had the means for instant gratification and fiscal irresponsibility. And since our family budget didn't allow for me to wear the latest brands or trends when I was growing up, that's exactly what I did – I started living beyond my means and making poor decisions regarding money. Was it just me? Unfortunately, I almost passed the same bad habits on to my daughter.

When my daughter was 5 years old, I made a "Rookie Mom" mistake. She asked me for money to spend at the school's Christmas Bazaar, where she could buy gifts for the family. So I handed a $20 bill to a kindergartner with the naïve expectation that she would make responsible purchases and bring back my change. When she came home later that day, my daughter proudly laid out her wares: a candy cane; a packet, not a box, of hot cocoa; a homemade, felt ornament; a snowflake made from glued popsicle sticks; and a slew of candy wrappers! When I asked her for my change, she dug into her pocket and pulled out $2.38. I couldn't even get mad. I had not taught her fiscal responsibility. I had not shown her faithfulness in money matters. I shook my head and told myself, "never again."

Like my daughter, and my young adult self, many of us have not learned the principles of faithfulness when it comes to money or other areas of our lives. But, Scripture tells us that when we are faithful – or responsible, consistent, and trustworthy – with a few things, God will readily bless us with more. The problem is that many of us have been just the opposite and have paid a steep price (no pun intended). Think about it. How many times have you gotten frustrated about things you don't have, but haven't stopped to appreciate the things you do have? Or, how many times have you prayed for increase, but haven't given thanks for current resources? If I'm honest, the answer is too many times. And this is how we end up living beyond our means and becoming the architects of our own poverty. Instead of utilizing the "robbing Peter to pay Paul" system of money management, we need to start trying to "make a dollar out of fifteen cents." Instead of buying more things and a larger home to put them in, we should donate those items we no longer wear or use, and bless someone in need.

This faith journey is going to require you to take inventory of what God has given you. It will require you to ask, "How can I best use the resources and talents that I've been blessed with?" instead of "How can I get more?" Sometimes when we see others with things we want, we are quick to question, "why them and not me?" But instead, we should ask ourselves, "Have I used what I have to meet the needs of others the same way God meets my daily needs?" We forget that God has blessed us to be a blessing, and not just to keep the blessings to ourselves.

Look at the parable of talents in the Gospel of Matthew.54 In this passage, a master praises two servants for their faithful use of monetary resources given them. But, the master chastises the third servant for not putting his resources to any good use. In fact, the master calls this third servant "wicked," "lazy," and "worthless," because the servant buried his talent in the ground. As such, the master took away his talent and cast him away.

Sadly, sometimes we act like the last servant, especially when what we have is not as much or as grand as what someone else has. We act like our talent is worthless or we take it for granted. As a result, we do not put to good use what we've been blessed with, and certainly do not please God. If you want more, start appreciating and maximizing the "less." Pray for wisdom to use the gifts that you have been given to serve God and others. I can testify that once you stop focusing on what you don't have and start being grateful for what you do have, you will experience blessings on blessings on blessings.

PRAY THIS

Lord, help me take inventory. Please reveal the gifts, the talents, and the time that I am not using to their greatest potential. Show me how to use these gifts in a way that You will get glory, so that You can trust me with more. Amen.

TWEET | POST THIS

The key to having more is maximizing "LESS."
#BelievingBigger31

---

54 Matthew 25:14-30

Believing Bigger: What gifts or talents have you buried? Why? How can you use them to serve God and His people?

"When I think about creating abundance, it's not about creating a life of luxury for everybody on this planet; it's about creating a life of possibility. It is about taking that which was scarce and making it abundant."

~ Peter Diamandis

14. HOW SOON WE FORGET

> *"He said to his disciples, 'Why are you so afraid? Do you still have no faith?'"*
> Mark 4:40

LeBron James is easily one of the most polarizing and maligned figures in sports. He garners the attention of those who love him and those who love to hate him. When he started his basketball career with the Cleveland Cavaliers, he quickly became a local phenomenon, and within five years, a global sensation. Sports pundits described him as a "force," a "freak of nature," and arguably one the greatest basketball players of all time. He was, and still is, often compared to basketball legend, Michael Jordan. And now, his net worth is just shy of $300 million from basketball earnings and a myriad of product endorsements.

But on July 8, 2010, LeBron went from a beloved hero to traitorous villain for many fans. Frustrated that he had not won a championship with his hometown team, Lebron, with the world watching, made the decision to take his talents to South Beach, Florida, to play for the Miami Heat. Cleveland fans cursed his name and burned his jersey in the streets. The team's owner wrote a public and scathing letter denouncing LeBron and attacking his character. Other players and sports pundits disdained him or questioned his ethics. Despite his consistent performance... despite the number of scoring records he had broken... despite the revenue he generated for the team and for Cleveland, none of it mattered. The people who had once praised and celebrated him, now questioned and doubted him.

I imagine this is how Jesus felt about His disciples. The Gospel of Mark recounts a time where, after a long day of teaching crowds by the seaside, Jesus fell asleep in the ship as He and the disciples traveled to the next location.[55] As Jesus slept, a great storm arose and massive waves crashed against the ship. The waves were so vicious that the ship filled with water and panic erupted like a volcano. But, in the midst of this chaos and turbulence, Jesus was sound asleep. Fearing for their lives, the disciples woke Him, accusing, "do you NOT CARE that we are perishing?" (Mark 4:38, emphasis added).

At this stage of Jesus' ministry, the disciples had seen Jesus perform no less than 10 miracles. By now, they had left behind friends, family, and fortunes to follow Him. They had never gone hungry. They were never without clothes and shelter. And though they were under constant threat and surveillance by Jewish leaders, they had never been in any real danger. Jesus had a spotless track record. If he were a basketball player, his game-winning shot would be clutch. He never missed. He had proven worthy of their trust and yet, when the storm came, they panicked.

And we do the very same thing when the inevitable storms of life arise. When faced with job loss, declining health, rebellious children, broken marriages, and unpaid bills, we cry out to God, "do you NOT CARE that I am suffering?!" We may wonder, "Jesus, are you asleep?" "Do you see what's going on down here?" "Did you hear what he just said to me?" "Do you know what she just did?" These questions exemplify the very heart of our humanity, reflecting our emotions, our fears and our frustrations. But they also reflect our lack of faith.

Just look at how Jesus responded when the disciples woke him up. He didn't freak out. He didn't get nervous. He didn't start trying to scoop water out of the ship. He spoke three, simple words, "Peace! Be still!" and immediately, the sea was calm. Jesus was

---

55 See Mark 4:35-41

not surprised by the storm. He knew it was coming before He set foot on the ship. He was not concerned because He also knew that He had the power to quiet the storm. Jesus knew this. But somehow, even after all that they had witnessed, all the ways Jesus had protected and provided for them, the disciples did not. So He turned to them, incredulously, and asked, "Why are you so afraid? Do you still have no faith?" (Mark 4:40).

In other words, Jesus wanted to know why they doubted Him after everything He had done and all the ways He cared for them. And He's asking us the same questions today.

When storms rise and winds blow in your life, it is easy to forget that the Lord is always there with you. Nothing can happen to you unless He permits it and there is no situation He is unable to calm. He is never surprised. And He is never caught off guard. Trials are inevitable in life. Sometimes God uses them to teach us, and other times to perfect our faith.[56] Your challenge on this faith journey is to remember that with **one word**, God has the power to calm the storm.

PRAY THIS

Lord, thank You for reminding me that You are in control, especially during times of storm. Lord, help me to have the same peace that You did, where I can rest knowing that with one word, You can bring about a change in my life. Amen.

TWEET|POST THIS

The winds and the waves still obey Him.
#BelievingBigger31

---

56 James 1:3

Believing Bigger: What storms has God brought you out of? How can you use that experience to strengthen your faith in the future?

"There is always a storm. There is always rain. Some experience it. Some live through it. And others are made from it."
~ Shannon Alder

15. THE COVER UP

> *"Where there is no guidance, a people falls, but in an abundance of counselors there is safety."*
> Proverbs 11:14

I'm a big fan of Starbucks – the brand, the merchandise, and their seasonal pecan tarts (yummy!), but I do not like, nor do I drink, coffee. Now don't get me wrong, I've tried espressos, lattes, flat-white, iced coffee, hot coffee, and coffee whipped with confections I can't even pronounce. But still, my relationship with coffee mirrors, "Sam I Am" from Dr. Seuss's Green Eggs and Ham.

Tea, on the other hand, is a different story. Be it herbal, chai, rooibos, green, or white, teas have been my go-to drink of choice.

My favorite is a honey-ginseng green tea from Panera. One morning, I stopped in for a cup before I began my work day. After getting my tea, I got back into the car and started my commute. Due to construction, I hit a few bumps, and despite there being a lid on the cup, several drops of tea spilled out and into the car. In that moment, I had a realization. Although the cup was covered, there was a scalding hot beverage just beneath the lid, and all it took for it to come to the surface was a few bumps in the road. So it is in life. When we get hurt, we mistakenly believe that just because we've put a "lid" on the pain – buried it, don't talk about it, covered it up, or masked it (hashtag #overit) – the issue has been contained. But when the bumps of life come, when our hurt gets triggered, when the emotions come flooding back, there will be some spillover.

My biggest "cover up" was the absence of my biological father. I never met him; he intentionally stayed away from me. But I was good. You can't miss what you've never had, right? For years, I thought I was over it. I had put on my big girl panties, soldiered on, and sucked it up. I had gone to college, gotten several degrees, had a blossoming career, and made a decent salary. But then I got married, and before long, my daddy issues came bubbling to the surface. I told myself, *"You can't depend on a man," "Don't expect a man to contribute," "You don't need a man to raise a child."* I thought that my hurts had been healed, but the truth is, I had just covered them up. When I was growing up, we didn't really talk about our feelings, so I knew no other way to cope but to bury them. And many of us are like this. We perpetuate a code of silence even though it is detrimental to our very existence.

Consider Alice Walker's *The Color Purple*. Celie was sexually abused by her stepfather, but warned that she "better not never tell nobody but God." That experience, was the catalyst for a pattern of domestic abuse that lasted well into her adult years.

So many of us, like Celie, are still carrying the scars of our own childhood. Despite our education, numerous accomplishments, professional expertise... Despite who we know or even what we have... we hinder our ability to thrive by trying to cover up our hurts.

When I became a mom, I realized this truth even more. I learned how important it is to fully deal with hurts and decided then to stop passing on the pathology of sucking it up and soldiering on. I wanted to teach my daughter that deep hurts need to be acknowledged in order to be healed. While the scars of my childhood caused me to be inherently distrustful of people, I knew that I would never be able to build a healthy marriage or family, and certainly not a successful business or lifestyle that served others, if I didn't deal with my childhood hurts.

Fortunately, the Bible provides direct instruction about how to deal with problems. The main lesson is realizing that we are not, and we do not have to deal with our struggles, alone. Psalm 55:22 says, "Cast your burden on the Lord and He will sustain you; he will never permit the righteous to be moved." In other words, we can take our concerns to the Lord who will give us the strength to press on. The other lesson, and this is a hard one for many, is knowing that it is ok and sometimes necessary to seek the wisdom of counselors.[57] I say that this one is hard because like me, many of you were taught that therapy is something for "bored housewives and rich, white folks." But that is a lie the enemy wants us to believe. We were never meant to bury pain and cover it up like it never happened.

Being brave doesn't mean pretending that it doesn't hurt.

Your faith journey is going to require you to make peace with your past. It will require you to be honest with yourself, and with God, because nothing is hidden from Him anyway.[58] It may cost you some tears and a few trips to the therapist, but that pales in comparison to what it will cost you in missed opportunities, healthy relationships, and the true peace of God if you don't deal with your hurts.[59] Don't be afraid to reach out to a licensed professional or spiritual counselor who shares your values. Ask God for the wisdom to find someone that can help you and for discernment in making your choice. He will.

---

57 Proverbs 11:14
58 Hebrews 4:13
59 Philippians 4:7

PRAY THIS

Lord, who am I fooling? You know the things and the people that have left scars and created wounds that have yet to heal. Lord, I release them to You, and pray that Your Holy Spirit brings closure, peace, and forgiveness. Amen.

TWEET|POST THIS

Man covers up, but Jesus covers all.
#BelievingBigger31

Believing Bigger: What is the Cover Up in your life? How is it hindering you? Who do you need to forgive or what might you need to heal, so that you can live freely?

"Forgiving does not erase the bitter past. A healed memory is not a deleted memory. Instead, forgiving what we cannot forget creates a new way to remember. We change the memory of our past into a hope for our future."
~ Lewis B. Smedes

16. BACKGROUND CHECK

> *"Therefore, if anyone is in Christ, he is a new creation. The old has passed away; behold the new has come."*
> *2 Corinthians 5:17*

In 1996, I packed my bags for college and headed off to campus as a new freshman with a scholarship in one hand and a criminal record in the other. The scholarship was a blessing; the criminal record was baggage. Going to college, let alone away to college was a tremendous privilege for me, especially considering the alternative – 3-5 years in state prison. Unfortunately, I was one of those girls you read about in the papers. I had a part-time job at a clothing store, and instead of doing an honest day's work for an honest day's pay, I got greedy. For a kid who never had the latest fashion or the newest gym shoes, and who envied the kids who had the means or the parents to buy them whatever they wanted, the temptation of working in a clothing store became too much for me to withstand. And I did what many of us do. I allowed myself to believe that if I had material wealth, status symbols, and "looked the part," I would be accepted, included, liked. Three days before my senior prom, my crimes caught up with me and I was escorted out of my job, handcuffed and humiliated.

Applying for jobs over the next few years was a nightmare. Whenever I came to the question, "have you ever been convicted?" My heart sank. My throat tightened. I would just ball up the application and throw it away. Being a successful and thriving college student, who had earned a merit-based scholarship, was evidence that I was turning my life around, but I was still haunted by the choices of my past. I was ashamed, and I judged myself more harshly than anyone else. Despite the fact that I was now making better choices and building healthy relationships, I was stuck in the past.

"Your background... it ain't squeaky clean. Shh... sometimes we all gotta swim upstream." Whenever I hear Jill Scott sing these words, I am reminded that we all have fallen short of the mark at some point in our lives. But, this age of social sharing would have us to believe that the picture perfect, digital portfolios of happy lives, thriving businesses, loving marriages, and perfect parents are real. If we're honest, though, we know that social media rarely tells all the news that's fit to post. **Public success and private mess** has become commonplace.

As I sat on campus, I realized that I had been fooling myself. Yes, I had been making better decisions. Yes, I had gotten good grades. And yes, I was forming bonds with people who would serve as positive influences in my life. But, who was I kidding? There was still one area in which I was just playing games. Even though I had been going to church since I was 9 or 10, I still had not truly given my life and my will over to God. I prioritized the approval and acceptance of other people above His.[60] I always wanted something "better" than what was right in front of me. I was ungrateful, unthankful, and unhappy with His blessings. And that's how I lived my life for more years than I care to admit. Looking back, I am amazed at how arrogant I was. The Bible says that "pride goes before destruction,"[61] and I was living proof.

By the time I had truly accepted God into my heart, and truly began to live for Him, I had years of destructive choices, hurt feelings, betrayed trust, and broken hearts to contend with. My past looked like the devastation of a small town after a tornado. How could one person cause so much damage? How could someone with my rap sheet be a light for anyone? Didn't that make me a hypocrite? But God spoke to me and reminded me

---

60 John 12:43
61 Proverbs 16:18

that He has removed my sins as far as the east is from the west.62 The old me began to die the moment I made a real commitment to live for Christ.

Your faith journey is going to require you to come to terms with your past and your present choices. If 2 Corinthians 5:17 is true, and we are new creations in Him, then our decisions, our actions, and our thoughts and desires should align with His will and His word. And while this makes the future exciting and hopeful, it doesn't erase the decisions we've made in the past or the consequences resulting from them. God's grace is sufficient to cover our sins, and He is faithful to forgive us,63 but we will still reap the seeds we've sown.64 Just like loving parents discipline their children, God corrects us in love.65 Thankfully, we do not receive all that we are due, but there are still repercussions we must deal with as we accept God's forgiveness.

As you begin to deal with your past choices and line up your life for the future God wants you to have, remember that there is nothing in your background that can prevent you from receiving Christ's love.66 God knew what you were capable of doing. In fact, He knew exactly what you would do every day of your life, and that is the very reason He created the ultimate restoration plan so that we would not suffer the full consequences for our mistakes.67 So as you embrace your calling to serve others, do not allow the mistakes of the past to hinder you. God's judgment reigns above all finger pointers, backbiters, shade throwers, and naysayers.68

---

62 Psalm 103:12
63 1 John 1:9
64 Galatians 6:7
65 Hebrews 12:6
66 Romans 8:38-29
67 John 3:16
68 Romans 8:33-34

PRAY THIS

Lord, I realize that sometimes the hardest person to forgive is myself. There are some things that I'm not particularly proud of, but I pray that You open my heart to receive Your forgiveness, strengthen my resolve to receive Your correction, and quiet the inner voice from my past that haunts me. Amen.

TWEET|POST THIS

The past doesn't have a forwarding address.
#BelievingBigger31

Believing Bigger: What do you need to leave in the past? How can you use that experience to help others learn a valuable lesson?

"Every man is guilty of all the good he did not do."
~ Voltaire

17. WHO CAN I RUN TO?

> *"But Jonah rose to flee to Tarshish from the presence of the Lord. He went down to Joppa and found a ship going to Tarshish. So he paid the fare and went down into it, to go with them to Tarshish, away from the presence of the Lord."*
> Jonah 1:3

In the modern age, corporal punishment of children is extremely frowned upon. Parents who physically discipline their children are often labeled violent or abusive, or both. But back in my day, disobedience meant there would be some consequences and repercussions. Discipline usually meant physical punishment with whatever was in arm's reach at the time of the infraction, including: house shoes, gym shoes, paint stirrers, extension cords, paddles, broom handles, belts, or Hot Wheels ™ race tracks. And when none of those things were available, a good, old-fashioned backhand would do the job. But times have changed and so has some people's approach to parenting. What has not changed is the growing pandemic of defiant children and the need for some type of disciplinary action.

Were you or are you one of those defiant kids? Have your parents ever asked you to do something and you just didn't do it? You didn't feel like it or didn't think it was a good idea. Whatever the reason, you chose to ignore your parents' admonitions. What happened? Did you suffer any consequences? Or, what about you parents? Have you ever asked your children to do something or not do something and they outright defied you? What about continually asking your child to do something, and they continually disobey you. What did you do? Were you inclined to take extreme and drastic measures like putting your son or daughter out of the house? Did you suspend privileges, shut off cable or other amenities, take away clothes you bought except five school outfits, or make your child sleep on the floor instead of the comfy mattress you purchased for him or her. Ok, maybe those last two were just my mom. But, you had to have done something, right? Because a defiant child, a willfully and persistently disobedient kid, is a parent's worst nightmare.

The back and forth struggle parents have with their children is a perfect illustration of our relationship with God. Not only do we have bouts of disobedience, not only are we defiant, but many of us are arrogant about it. Whether we do things we aren't supposed to do, or refuse to do the things He asks us to do, we have the nerve, the arrogance to expect Him to keep paying our bills, to keep maintaining our health, to keep providing food, shelter, and clothing. We expect Him to keep blessing us. But, imagine your child, who has just outright defied you, turning around and asking you to pay his or her cell phone bill, or requesting money for a new pair of shoes? Would he have any teeth left? Mmm hmm. Thought so.

Fortunately, God does not always give us the punishment our actions deserve,[69] but He does respond. Look at what happened to Jonah.[70] God told Jonah to go and preach to the residents of Nineveh; Jonah refused. In fact, he more than refused; he put 2,500 miles of distance between himself and Nineveh, by fleeing to Tarshish. Jonah didn't want to minister to the residents of Nineveh because they were Assyrians, an idolatrous people and a dangerous threat to Israel. Jonah thought they deserved whatever punishment they had coming; he knew that if he went to Nineveh and they believed, God would not lay the smack down. Jonah had assigned *himself* judge, jury, and executioner. Disobedient. Defiant. Arrogant.

God could have killed him, but He decided to handle things

69 Romans 6:23
70 See Jonah 1-4

differently. He put Jonah in "time out." In fact, God is the creator of the "time out." When Jonah jumped on a ship to flee from God, God sent a violent storm to get his attention. As the waves crashed into the boat, the seamen tried to row back to shore, but it was no use. God sent more waves, more violent than before. When they realized that Jonah was the cause of the calamity, they tossed him overboard, and the sea immediately became calm. Jonah did not drown, but found himself in a time out... three days and three nights in the belly of a fish. During his time out, Jonah realized who the real God was and cried out to Him. God responded and gave Jonah another chance to obey. This time, Jonah did as he was told.

Just like Jonah, your faith journey is going to require you to do some things that you don't want to do. It may require you to drive into some areas that don't valet. It may cause you to build bridges when you'd rather build walls. It will definitely require you to stay in your lane, heed God's instruction, and set aside your will for His. This is because the consequences of disobedience affect more than just you. See how the seamen suffered because Jonah didn't want to act right? Other people are also impacted by your response to God. Think about bitter mothers who rob their children of a relationship with their father because they can't forgive him for the breakup. God tells us to love our enemy, to pray for those who are mean and spiteful,[71] but sometimes we'd rather see them burn. God tells us to forgive[72] when we'd rather hold a grudge. But remember, our job is not to punish.[73] Our job is simply to obey. You can run like Jonah, but just as he could not hide from God, neither can you. So, if God is calling you to serve, to forgive, or submit to

71 Matthew 5:44
72 Colossians 3:13
73 Romans 12:19

His will, just do it. Don't be one of His kids who has to learn the hard way.

PRAY THIS

Lord, even though I may be reluctant, give me a heart of obedience to do what You have called me to do. Move my will out of the way so that others might be blessed. Help me to understand that my obedience is the key to someone else's breakthrough. Amen.

TWEET|POST THIS

I'm not on the run. I'm ready for duty.
#BelievingBigger31

Believing Bigger: What has God been calling you to do that you're running from or uncomfortable doing? Have you assigned yourself judge, jury or executioner? What can you do to make things right?

"You cannot escape the responsibility of tomorrow by evading it today."
~ Abraham Lincoln

18. WHO ME?

> *"But Moses pleaded with the Lord, 'O Lord, I'm not very good with words. I never have been, and I'm not now, even though you have spoken to me. I get tongue-tied, and my words get tangled.'" Exodus 4:10* [74]

Imagine heading out to your favorite coffee shop one afternoon. It's a nice day, so you decide to walk. As you breathe in the fresh air, enjoying the warmth of the sun on your face, your daydreaming is interrupted by a piercing scream, "HELP!" You frantically look in each direction until you spot a woman, a block ahead, struggling with a man trying to snatch her purse. Instinctively, you reach for your phone to call the police. Just then, a squad car pulls up to the stop sign on the corner where you are standing.

"Thank God!" You sigh. Then pointing to the scene ahead, you exclaim, "Officer, that woman is being robbed!" The officer nods in polite acknowledgment and then, to your surprise, turns his vehicle to drive in the opposite direction, as the woman lays on the ground and the assailant runs away with her purse.

How would you feel? Shocked? Angry? Afraid? Would you sympathize with the woman who is now sobbing into her hands feeling alone and helpless? Would you file a complaint? How would this shape your perception of law enforcement? The justice system? First responders?

If you answered that you'd be angry and indignant, you are not alone. Many of us would feel that way. After all, it was the officer's duty to help that woman. He had taken an oath to protect and serve the public, so how could he, in a person's time of need, *blatantly* turn a blind eye? Sure, you also could have attempted to help, but you're not trained to fight crime. You don't have the same expertise, and the robber could have had a weapon – a gun, a knife, anything. Ultimately, that situation is exactly the type that the officer had been trained to respond to.

If your confidence in law enforcement is already shaken, then consider a doctor who sits by watching while a choking victim loses consciousness... or a fireman who sits on his truck, unbothered, while a nearby house is ablaze. It seems incredulous to think that someone who has made a *commitment* to serve, and is *equipped* to do so, would choose not to. And yet, as Christians, we do it all the time. When God calls us to serve, to lead, to take up our crosses and follow Him daily,[74] we have all kinds of excuses for not doing it:

"See, the way my life is set up, I can't..." "Well, if I didn't have this tricky knee..." "Missionary?!
Chile please! I will barely go out of state!" "I just got this new job..." "I just started school..."
"Hmmm... let me pray about it..."

Our responsibility as Christians is great and the impact of our service, or lack thereof, is real. A woman who loses her purse in a robbery can have her belongings restored. A person who loses consciousness while choking can be revived. And a house that has been burned to ash can be rebuilt. But what happens when a woman's hope runs out? More, importantly, what happens when someone dies without having had an opportunity to gain salvation? Our call to serve, to lead, and to love affects real people and makes a real difference. So what is it that prevents us from fulfilling the call? What stops us from rendering service when we see an unmet need?

For Moses, it was that he thought he was unqualified. When God called Moses to lead the children of Israel out of captivity, Moses'

---

74 New Living Translation

first instinct was to try to duck out of it. Moses gave every excuse in the book – who am I to talk to Pharaoh? What if they ask who You are God? What if they don't believe me? I'm not good with words.[75] But God reassured Moses and **insisted** that he fulfill the task. Think about that. The God of the universe could have chosen *anybody*, especially since Moses was literally begging God to send someone else, but He chose Moses. And He equipped Moses with everything he would need for the assignment. God even allowed Aaron to accompany Moses on the journey to give Moses peace of mind. Though Moses felt unqualified, though he thought someone else was better for the task, God knew that Moses was perfectly suited and perfectly positioned to be successful.

Just like Moses, we often underestimate our true value. We measure our worth by what we have, where we went go to school, or with whom we've rubbed elbows. But God's very *specific* plan for your life does not use the same measuring stick. God doesn't compare you to everyone else. He doesn't treat you like a commodity. He did not create you in assembly line fashion or as a carbon copy of everyone else. God created you uniquely, meticulously, so when He calls you to serve, lead, or to minister, it's because He knows your full potential. Think about it: who knows what will work for you better than the One who made you? God would not call you to do something that He was not 100% confident you could handle.

Your faith journey is going to require you to look beyond your personal limitations, and see the needs of people who are waiting to be freed. God called you to a specific task for a specific reason. He didn't ask just anyone to do it. He asked **you.** Think about what would have happened if Moses had

---

75 Exodus 3:11, 13; 4:1, 10

not been obedient. Millions of people would have been left in captivity. And the same may be true with you. There are those who are depending on you to heed God's calling on your life so that they can be freed from their imprisonment. Captivity is not limited to physical confinement. It includes mental and emotional bondage, depression, insecurity, addictions, cycles of violence, abuse, promiscuity, gang involvement, corruption, and the list goes on and on... Just like the police officer, the fire fighter, and the doctor, you are duty bound to serve, and became so the moment you accepted Christ as Lord and Savior. Don't let insecurity and fear be the reason someone stays in captivity. Remember the joy you felt when you were freed from your situation? Help someone else get there.

PRAY THIS

Lord thank you for setting me free. Thank you for sending caring people into my life to show me the way to you. Please help me to do the same for someone else. In Jesus Name, Amen.

TWEET |POST THIS

God freed me to free others.
#BelievingBigger31

Believing Bigger: Do you have a testimony about being freed from captivity? Recall it and share it. How did your life change after you were freed? How can your testimony free others?

"Doing nothing for others is the undoing of ourselves."
~ Horace Mann

19. STAY IN YOUR LANE

> *"And Sarai said to Abram, 'Behold now, the Lord has prevented me from bearing children. Go in to my servant; it may be that I shall obtain children by her.' And Abram listened to the voice of Sarai."*
> Genesis 16:2

If there is one vice that has plagued me from my youth until now, it is impatience. I hate to wait. I mean I hate it! If something I want isn't happening fast enough, I try my best to make it happen on my own. And because God loves me enough to let me make my own decisions, er... mistakes, He steps back, and says, "OK, honey. You go right on ahead."

Suffice it to say, the results have been disastrous. You would think that I would have learned my lesson but, unfortunately, I was one of those kids who had to repeat some classes more than once.

I have since learned that impatience is a dangerous cocktail of doubt, fear, arrogance, and pride – four attributes that God absolutely despises. [77] And it is an indirect way of telling God:

"I don't trust you." "No. I got this."
"You're not moving fast enough."
"MY way is just as good as your way."

The truth is, as believers, our spirit is always at war with our flesh.[78] We are in a constant tug-of-war between what we want and what God wants for us. Sometimes we think it's hard to tell which is which, but it's really quite simple. Your flesh seeks instant gratification and is driven by things like greed, lust, pride, and selfishness. Here are some examples. A woman who pressures her child's father into marriage so she can swap out the "baby mama" title for a more respectable title of "wife," is operating out of pride. Missing quality time with your children to work extra hours for

---

77 James 1:6-7; 2 Timothy 1:7; Proverbs 16:18
78 Ephesians 6:12

unnecessary, material items is the manifestation of greed. Posting suggestive pictures on social media to get people to "like" you is a form of lust. Paying to get your "hair done, nails done, everything did," when there's a stack of unpaid bills hidden in your kitchen drawer is selfish and plain irresponsible. Whenever we choose to act recklessly, whenever we choose not to wait on God's provision and, instead, take matters into our own hands, there is always a steep price to pay.

Look at what happened to Abraham and his wife, Sarah.[79]

God told Abraham that he would be a father with many descendants,[80] but when a decade had passed, and Sarah had not produced any children, she decided to take matters into her own hands (Genesis 16:2-3). To be barren in a society that revered mothers was difficult. Couples who were able to bear children, especially male children, boasted of their legacy and the continuation of the family bloodline. Because of this, a wife that could not bear her husband any children felt shame.

To complicate matters, Sarah's biological clock was ticking. She and Abraham were getting beyond traditional childbearing years. Out of desperation, Sarah suggested that her husband have children through her servant, Hagar.

If you resonate with Sarah's dilemma, it's likely because you have experienced a version of it. God promised you something. You received the promise with joy. Time passed. More time passed. Even more time passed. And at some point, you got discouraged. Your faith started to wane as you noticed how many other people seemed to be getting exactly what God had promised you. Your Facebook timeline was full of friends posting about how

---

79 Please note that the beginning of the events referenced in this chapter occurred before God renamed Abram to Abraham, and Sarai to Sarah in Genesis 17:5, 15; however, for ease of reference, I will use Abraham and Sarah throughout.

80 Genesis 15:5

God had blessed them, as you waited patiently for God to do the same for you. So, like Sarah, you decided to speed up the timetable, aggressively trying to manufacture what God had already promised was on the way. Maybe you were not trying to have a child, but maybe it was a house, a car, a new job, a spouse, or a person with "spouse potential"... Whatever it was, you decided that enough was enough, and you were going to "go get your blessing." Since God had already said it was yours, you rationalized, like Sarah did, that your efforts to aid God in the process were technically okay. Right?

As believers, we have to understand that God has a will, but He also has a way. Just because God allows us to have free will, does not mean we should abuse the liberty,[81] or that He needs help being God. I don't know how your predicament turned out, but I'm sure it wasn't much better than Abraham's and Sarah's situation.

Abraham listened to Sarah, slept with Hagar, and Hagar got pregnant [with Ishmael](Genesis 16:4). That's when things went from bad to worse! Hagar, "the side chick" started acting like she was "the main chick", taunting and mistreating Sarah; Sarah snapped on Abraham and told him that this was his fault; Abraham got frustrated and told Sarah to deal with it; and ultimately Hagar ran away (16:5-6).

All of this happened because Abraham and Sarah decided to interfere with God's timing. Despite their impatience, God did fulfill his promise to Abraham and Sarah; together they conceived and gave birth to a son, Isaac,[82] but the damage had already been done. Even today, the descendants of Ishmael and Isaac are still in conflict over who is the rightful heir of Abraham's

---

81 1 Corinthians 10:23
82 Genesis 21:1-2

inheritance.[83]

Your faith journey is going to test the limits of your patience. When you try to manufacture the outcome, instead of trusting God's timing for your blessings, you will create unnecessary problems for yourself and those around you. Think about it, isn't a cake made from scratch with fresh, high quality ingredients cooked to perfection in an oven better than an instant, store bought cake-in-a-box zapped in someone's microwave? Of course it is.

But, the homemade cake takes time, and we have to patiently wait for its goodness. In the same way, we have to stop trying to rush God's promises because we end up settling for half-baked blessings. Instead let's wait for God's handcrafted creation, made with love especially for us.

PRAY THIS

Lord, forgive me for being impatient. Thank you, for showing me that not waiting on you is a sign of mistrust and insecurity. Give me the strength to wait and the peace of knowing that when my blessing arrives, it will be everything I need it to be.

Amen.

TWEET | POST THIS

I'll wait.

#BelievingBigger31

---

83 Genesis 21:10

Believing Bigger: Can you think of a time when your impatience got the better of you? What did you learn from that experience? What was at the root of your impatience?

"Patience is bitter, but its fruit is sweet."
~ Jean Jacque Rousseau

20. CONSIDER YOUR WAYS

> *"Now this is what the Lord Almighty says: '*
> *Give careful thought to your ways.*
> *You have planted much, but harvested little.*
> *You eat, but never have enough.*
> *You drink, but never have your fill.*
> *You put on clothes, but are not warm.*
> *You earn wages, only to put them in a purse with holes in it.'"*
> *Haggai 1:5-6*

I've been blessed to build a business that has equipped thousands of entrepreneurs with the strategies to create, launch, and grow their own brands. I've taught people how to do things like: develop and grow their platform, design systems, compose teams, generate content and maximize social media strategies that are proven methods for success. Yet, despite all of the tools, tips, checklists, and how-tos, there is one major factor that I am unable to influence or devise a strategy to overcome:

The Will of God. While I have been blessed to attract clients who profess faith in Christ, I cannot tell just from looking at or talking with them whether their business plans are in line with God's perfect will for their lives.

God's perfect will is very different from God's permissive will. God's perfect will connects His divine plan, that He revealed in His Word, with our obedience to that plan, while His permissive will refers to those things that God allows to happen even though they may not line up with His divine plan. Let me use an illustration from my life to show you the difference.

When I went to college, I was determined to have a career in law enforcement. In fact, I wanted to be an undercover narcotics officer, or a federal agent with the DEA (Drug Enforcement Administration). Despite my intentions, I met obstacle after obstacle as I attempted to move forward with my plan. At every turn, there was some barrier or hindrance indicating that I was on the wrong path. I felt like I was driving a car and getting caught at every red light. Clearly, my plan did not line up with God's perfect will. But, God did not prevent me from pursuing this path or demand that I submit to his call to go in a different direction. He permitted me to make my own decisions about my major and career options. Though God permitted me to follow my own course, after hitting enough roadblocks, I realized that I needed to reevaluate. I had made plans without once asking God what I should do and if law enforcement was the right path for me. After praying, I ultimately decided to alter course. I'll be honest; I was not at all happy about it and I grudgingly made the switch. But, as soon as I did, everything started to fall into place. Doors flung open left and right. People were literally coming out of the woodwork to help, hire, and mentor me. I received numerous opportunities to teach and to lead, which I likely would not have been able to do if I had continued to pursue my own agenda. Looking back, it is clear that God knew what was best. God knew that teaching was my gift, but He was not going to force me into it. Of course, He could have. But God doesn't work that way. Whenever we think that we know better than He does, He will step back and let us prove ourselves wrong. This was the case in the book of Haggai.[84] In this short book of the Bible, God specifically asked the people to rebuild His temple, but they put it on the back burner, deciding instead to chase money and pursue worldly affairs. Rather than build God's temple, they wanted to build their own empires. Having just been released from captivity in Babylon, you would think that serving God would have been the people's first priority. But it wasn't. They prioritized their economic development over their spiritual obedience. As a

---

84 See Haggai 1-2

result, God allowed the very thing that they were trying to avoid to happen. The people were trying to build up riches and live lavishly, so God called for a drought to prevent agricultural growth, the source of the people's wealth and well-being (Haggai 1:11). **God sent Haggai to challenge the people to consider what had occurred. They planted a lot, but yielded a small harvest. They ate, but were not full. They drank, but were still thirsty. They had clothes on, but were still cold. They made money, but were still poor (1:6).**

Sound familiar? How many of us have jobs, but can't seem to pay the bills? How many of us fear not having enough food to feed our families, and yet throw out massive amounts of unconsumed groceries? How many of us have closets full of clothes, but want more? Do you really need another pair of shoes, another sweater, another pair of slacks? The pursuit of these things has left many of us with massive credit card debt, trapped in jobs we hate, and worried about losing it all. God is telling us now as He did back then, "give careful thought to your ways." It is a bitter pill to swallow, but oftentimes we build our own prisons by prioritizing the pursuit of material success over God's will.

Your faith journey is going to require you to take a step back and do exactly what Haggai admonishes, give careful thought to where God falls on your priority list. If the first thing you reach for in the morning is your cell phone or the remote control instead of The Word or your daily devotion, consider your ways. If you are "too tired" to go to church on Sunday morning (#pjsallday), but have energy to go work, the movies, dinner with friends, and workout at the gym, consider your ways. If the thought of tithing 10% of your paycheck to the Lord is something you can't afford, but you pay the same amount on credit card minimums, consider your ways. God will permit you to live and die by your own choices. However, if you want to be in perfect alignment with His will, where your gifts, talents, abilities and wealth pursuits align with His word, consider your ways.

PRAY THIS

Lord, as I give careful thought to my ways, please reveal everything that I have given priority over you. Please help me to discern roadblocks from stepping-stones and let me yield to your perfect will instead of stumbling over my own way. In Jesus Name, Amen.

TWEET | POST THIS

I will. His will.
#BelievingBigger31

Believing Bigger: Evaluate where you are in life vs. where you want or where you thought you'd be. What is preventing you from being where you want to be? Now, consider, where God is on your list. What is preventing you from putting Him first? What changes do you need to make in order to correct this?

"If we command our wealth, we shall be rich and free; if our wealth commands us, we are poor indeed."
~Edmund Burke

21. ALL I DO IS WIN... NO MATTER WHAT[85]

> *"No, in all these things we are more than conquerors through him who loved us."*
> Romans 8:37

On May 8, 2014, with three seconds left in the fourth quarter and the score tied 96 – 96, the Chicago Bulls, who had been in a dogfight against LeBron James and the Cavs, had final possession of the ball. Shooting guard, Mike Dunleavy, frantically searching for an open man to inbound the ball, finds and passes the ball to Derrick Rose. Now, with just 1.8 seconds left on the clock, Derrick hoisted up a 21-foot jumper. In that moment, 23,000 fans in a sold out United Center and millions viewing from home fell silent as the ball soared, in what seemed like slow motion, toward the basket. The final buzzer echoed throughout the stadium as the ball miraculously found its way into the basket... Nothing. But. Net!

I didn't realize that I hadn't been breathing, but with ball in the net, the game over, and a Bulls victory, I felt like I had been shocked back to life. I hopped off the couch like a kangaroo and commenced to scream, fist bump, and happy dance my way all over the house. Although the Bulls would go on to lose the series, it was one of the most electrifying wins, and moral victories, of the season. I distinctly remember the anxiety, the uncertainty, and the nail biting during each moment of that game. Watching an epic battle between two dominant forces, and not knowing the outcome, was nerve-wracking.

For a sports fan, spoiling the outcome of a game is tantamount to treason; part of the fun is in *not knowing*. But as Christians, knowing the outcome is what keeps us sane during difficult times. As believers, we don't have to wait on the edge of our seats to see

---

85 Lyrics by DJ Khaled

who will get the victory. We already know that when challenges arise, the deck is stacked in our favor. We can celebrate because we know that God always causes us to triumph.[86] Now that's *Good News*, especially when you are in the midst of trying times and constantly facing persecution. Persecution practically defined the early church.[87] No one knew this better than Saul the Slayer who persecuted more than his fair share of Christians before he encountered Jesus and became known as the Apostle Paul.[88] Being a Christian in those days was about as popular as rain at a picnic. It was a no-no, a taboo. You may have a hard time understanding what life was like for Jesus' early followers because, in America, we have the privilege of religious freedom. We get to worship who we want, where we want, and when we want. But, that was not the case for those in the early church who preached the gospel of Jesus. They faced stoning, lynching, and crucifixion, just for their worship.[89] Even now, there are parts of the world where Christians are targeted and killed for their beliefs.

Physical harm, risk of imprisonment, and death threats are enough to make anyone question, even abandon their faith. Look at the things plaguing our nation right now. Too many innocent people are being slaughtered by gun violence. Children are losing their lives in record numbers. Soldiers feel safer at war than they do walking the streets of their own neighborhoods. Political corruption is at heights not seen since the days of Caesar. And while greed rises, compassion plummets. The weight of these hardships might leave your faith in shambles and questioning God, but the Apostle Paul offers us a different set of questions to consider:

---

86 2 Corinthians 2:14
87 Acts 7
88 Acts 9:1-22
89 Acts 7:54-60

o   *What shall we say in response to these things? If God is for us, who can be against us? (Romans 8:31)*

o   *Who will bring any charge against those whom God has chosen? It is God who justifies. (8:33)*

o   *Who shall separate us from the love of Christ? Shall trouble or hardship or persecution or famine or nakedness or danger or sword? (8:35)*

The answer to that last question is a resounding, "NO!" Despite the casualties lost during the battle, in the end, WE WIN the war (8:37). Victory is certain. It is guaranteed. These trials and setbacks are only temporary and cannot compare to the long-term victory we have with Jesus (8:18)

This faith journey will lead you through some trying times, and some nail biting experiences. But, take heart in knowing that the fight is fixed! The victory is already won! So there is no need to worry, and we don't have to be anxious. Jesus took the game winning shot on the cross of Calvary. He's the real MVP!

PRAY THIS

Lord, thank you for reminding me that in you, I have already overcome. Thank you for the victory. Give me the strength to hold on during the battle and give me the heart to praise you in the midst of difficult times.

In Jesus Name,

Amen.

TWEET | POST THIS

While I'm trying to figure it out, He's already worked it out.

#BelievingBigger31

Believing Bigger: Reflect on a victory that came through hardship. What do you think God was trying to teach you in that experience?

"I am not a victim. No matter what I have been through, I'm still here.
I have a history of victory."
~ Steve Maraboli

22. DIVINE DISAPPOINTMENT

"You do not have, because you do not ask."
James 4:2b

Although I have no recollection of it, my mother told me that she once broke up with a boyfriend because he promised to get me a "Toss Across" game for Christmas, but did not deliver. When she told me the story, I didn't think much of it. Actually, I didn't think it was a severe enough crime to end a relationship, but she was adamant. She said, "No ma'am. You don't make promises to *my child* and don't keep them!"

Now that I am a mother, I completely get it. She did not want me to grow up depending on unreliable people.

She wanted me to learn that people need to be accountable for their actions, and not to make commitments they don't intend to keep. Unfortunately, some of us know people who are exactly like that or, God forbid, you may even be those people. You know the ones I'm talking about... the ones who promise to take the little ones out for ice cream, to the amusement park, or on a special vacation... the ones who promise to show up for a child's school recital, birthday party, or special event... the ones who promise to love, honor and cherish 'til death do you part but, for one reason or another, they or we did not follow through. Regardless of who is at fault, the result is the same: disappointment. And when you've been disappointed enough times, you change.

If we're not careful, disappointment can interfere with numerous aspects of our lives. It can make us bitter and cynical. It can make us judge innocent people for disappointment caused by someone else. It can make us keep others at arms length, or make us petty and spiteful. And, it can make us too proud to ask for help when we need it. Worst of all, it can make you put God in the same category as those who have disappointed you in the past. If we're being honest, sometimes the reason that we don't pray like we should or ask God for the desires of our heart is because we don't want to be disappointed...again. But God is not a man that He would lie,90 and He does not make promises that he cannot keep.91

Some of us still do not trust God with our dreams, desires, or wishes. We don't want to hear, "No" or "Not yet."

But, think about it. What good parent gives their children *everything* they ask for? When a loving parent says, "No," there's a reason;

it is not an arbitrary response. It could be that the parent, being older and wiser, knows that the child is not ready, mature enough, or responsible enough to receive what he or she has asked for. Or, maybe, the thing requested has hidden dangers that the child is unaware of. Does saying "No" make the parent unfit, unfair, or unloving? Of course not. It's quite the contrary! It's called good parenting.

So why don't we hear God's "No" the same way?

Why don't we assume that our all-knowing, all-wise God has a legitimate reason for saying, "No"? Why don't we trust Him?

Even the child who has heard a parent say, "No," though disappointed, ultimately believes the parent still loves them.

That's because along with the "No's", the child has been consistently nurtured, cared for, loved and received blessings too numerous to count. Hasn't God been just as consistent with us?

The key to getting what we ask from God lies in our motivation, our intentions, and how well our request aligns with His will. When we ask for things that satisfy selfish ambitions, including frivolous

---

90 Numbers 23:19
91 2 Peter 3:9

purchases, God is not likely to answer affirmatively.92 Consider that. God knows the true intentions of our hearts, what really motivates us, and what we will do if He gives us what we ask for. He also knows whether the thing we ask for is best for us. Honestly, I am grateful God didn't give me everything I've asked for. God's "NOs" have allowed me to dodge so many bullets over the years. Now, as I've grown in His word, I pray for things that line up with His will for my life. For example, instead of asking for wealth, I ask Him for the discipline to live within my means and eliminate debt.93 Instead of asking for fame, I ask that He direct me to the opportunities that will give Him glory and minister to the people that need it most.94

Your faith journey is going to challenge you to examine the desires of your heart. Do you desire worldly wealth and popularity? Are you convinced that money equals security? Do you secretly covet the praise of others? (i.e. "You did that!") Until we recognize that our requests must line up with God's will, we will continue to experience the disappointment of God's "No." When we learn to find lasting satisfaction in the things of God, instead of the fleeting pleasures of the world, God will happily grant whatever we ask.95

---

92 James 4:3-4
93 Proverbs 22:7
94 John 21:17
95 Psalm 37:4; John 14:13

PRAY THIS

*Lord, thank you for loving me enough NOT to give me everything
that I ask for. Forgive me for putting human disappointment
on the same level as divine disappointment.
Thank you for having my back. Amen*

TWEET | POST THIS

When God says, "NO", He sees something I didn't.
Please and Thank you.
#BelievingBigger31

Believing Bigger: What is it that you really want from God, but may be afraid to ask? How will granting your request bring others to Christ or help someone in need?

"Disappointment to a noble soul is what cold water is to burning metal; it strengthens, tempers, intensifies, but never destroys it."
~ Eliza Tabor Stephenson

23. I FORGIVE YOU

> *"But go, tell his disciples and Peter that he is going before you to Galilee. There you will see him, just as he told you."*
> Mark 16:7

Often when I hear other believers share their testimony about the goodness of God and how He has shown them favor, they also mention how "unworthy" they are to receive God's blessing in the first place. Sometimes this is said to affirm the Scripture that we all have sinned and fallen short of God's glory;96 but, sometimes I hear something else in their voice… something that says, "I messed up so badly that I can't believe that God would forgive me." Moment of Truth: most believers are dealing with some form of sin in their lives. Even the Apostle Paul, one of the strongest examples of God's power to transform lives, struggled with sin.97 You are not alone. The problem is that when we sin, especially when we do it knowingly, willingly, and blatantly,the conviction and guilt we feel afterwards makes us feel like outcasts.

That can make it hard for us to seek God's forgiveness. And that is a dangerous place to be. In fact, it is exactly where the devil wants us to be. If Satan had his way, we would be so overcome by the guilt and shame resulting from our sin that we would start doubting ourselves, doubting whether God can love someone like us, and doubting whether Christ's love can cover sins like ours. That's why he gets in our mind to feed us lies like, "God will never forgive that!" "You're such a hypocrite. You never really changed!" "You're not a real Christian. You're a fake, a phony, a pretender." These lies are part of his plan to get you to stop praying, stop going to church, stop serving in ministry, and to start to isolating yourself from other believers. Satan is the classic abuser.

---

96 Romans 3:23
97 Romans 7:19

During my junior year of college, I completed a 6-month internship as a counselor in a shelter for battered women and children. One of the most powerful tricks of an abuser is isolating the victim from family, friends, and support systems. The goal is to sever those relationships so that the abuser can dominate and control his victim without prying eyes or accountability for his actions. And that's exactly what the enemy tries to do with us.

But God has a different plan. Look at Jesus' relationship with Peter. The night Jesus was taken away to be put on trial before his crucifixion, he had a conversation with His disciples, including Peter, one of His most trusted.[98] Peter was a soldier. He was a loud mouth, big brother kind of guy that you'd want with you on the playground at 3:00 if the school bully had challenged you to a fight. He was a part of Jesus' inner circle and a devoted friend. Yet, during their conversation, Jesus told Peter that before the rooster crowed at sunrise the next day, Peter would deny any association with Him.

Of course Peter tried to assure Him, even going so far as to say that he was ready to die with Jesus. But 40 verses later, Peter did exactly what Jesus said he would do.[99] Fearing for his own life, Peter denied having known Jesus at all, not once but three times. When Peter realized what he had done, he "wept bitterly." Peter wasn't just upset; he was distraught. Can you imagine the guilt he felt? Can you imagine what he was thinking? The shame? The weight of his actions on him? I mean this was Jesus, his boy…his brother! Peter had left everything to follow Him.

He had seen Jesus perform countless miracles, heal thousands, and was even there at Jesus' transfiguration, when He spoke to Moses and Elijah. This was the same Jesus that had invited Peter to

98 See Matthew 26:31-35
99 Matthew 26:75

walk on water, and saved him when he started to sink. Peter didn't just know Jesus; he loved Jesus and honored Him. Yet, in Jesus' hour of need, he bailed.

How would you feel? How could you live with yourself after that? And yet, that is exactly why Jesus came. He knew that Peter was going to sin just like He knew you were going to sin; and He still went to the cross as a sacrifice for Peter's sins and yours too. When Jesus said, "It is finished"[100], He was saying that He had completed the work He had been sent here to do, to die in Peter's place, your place, and my place, and to give us all a way to be reconciled to God.

Jesus had foretold that Peter would have a prominent role in the building of His church,[101] but with his betrayal, I am sure that Peter was thinking that all bets were off. But Jesus didn't count Peter out. In fact, Jesus wanted to be sure that Peter knew that he was still thought of as family. So, when Mary Magdalene, Mary the mother of James, and Salome went to anoint Jesus' body in the tomb, and the angel told the women that Jesus had risen, the angel gave Peter a special shout out.[102] He said to the women, "But go, tell his disciples and Peter that he is going before you to Galilee. There you will see him, just as he told you" (Mark 16:7). Why did he single out Peter? I imagine that in his depression, Peter thought he was no longer worthy to be called a disciple of Jesus, but Jesus wanted to make sure that Peter knew he was still loved,
he was still accepted, he was forgiven.

During your faith journey, you may experience guilt or shame because of the mistakes you've made in your past, and in your present. There will be moments where you will feel that God is

---

100 John 19:30
101 Matthew 16:13-18
102 See Mark 16:1-7

looking at you with the side eye. And there will be times that you are reluctant to seek His forgiveness because you think that what you've done is unforgiveable. But just like Peter, your sin debt has already been paid. Just like Peter, Jesus is saying to you, "You are forgiven." So, don't walk around burdened with shame. Jesus loves you. Love yourself enough to accept His forgiveness.

PRAY THIS
Lord, the struggle is real. I know I am far from perfect and sometimes I wonder how you can still love me after the things I think, do, and say. But Lord I thank you for your forgiveness. I accept it. I need it. I love you.
Amen.

TWEET | POST THIS
When I Forgive, I am FREE to Live.
#BelievingBigger31

Believing Bigger: Is there unconfessed or unresolved sin that is keeping you from truly serving God? Are you plagued by guilt or shame? Confess it to God. Free yourself and accept the peace of His forgiveness.

"To be a Christian means to forgive the inexcusable because
God has forgiven the inexcusable in you."
~ C. S. Lewis

24. I'M GOING DOWN

> *But when he saw the wind, he was afraid, and beginning to sink he cried out, 'Lord, save me.'"*
> *Matthew 14:30*

On New Year's Day, you commit to losing 20lbs, but the day you return to work, someone brings in a tray full of donuts. You promise you will stop cursing, but three days later, someone cuts you off in traffic, and makes you miss your turn. You decide it's finally time to give up smoking. The next day, all of the servers at work crash simultaneously, and the project you've been working on is lost. Isn't it amazing how every time you endeavor to make positive, healthy changes in your life, something comes along to derail your progress? By contrast, think about how little resistance you face while becoming addicted to food, alcohol, nicotine, or a sedentary lifestyle. It's not hard to overeat. It's not hard to over indulge in booze or cigarettes. And it's not hard to post up on the couch instead of hitting the gym.

Likewise, have you ever noticed how easy it is to focus on negative things instead of looking on the bright side? We tend to have more faith in all of the things that can go wrong than we do in the things that can go right. Even the disciples were guilty of this. In Matthew 14,[103] Jesus wanted to spend some time alone praying. So, He sent the disciples ahead of Him in the boat. When He had finished praying, the boat was a considerable distance away, so Jesus started to walk on the water towards the disciples and the boat. When they saw Jesus walking towards them, they immediately assumed the worst. "It's a ghost!" they cried out. Jesus tried to reassure them that He was not a ghost, but Peter was skeptical. "Lord, if it's you, tell me to come to you on the water." And Jesus

---

103 See Matthew 14:22-31

did. Peter walked on the water to meet Jesus, but when he saw the wind and the waves, he panicked and began to sink.

Now all of this happened right after Jesus had fed a multitude with two fish and five loaves of bread. The disciples had seen Jesus perform other miracles and healings, and had been with Him as He taught. But, despite Jesus' impeccable track record, the disciples – just like us – still struggled with fear and doubt. They were afraid because they had never seen a man walk on water. Likewise, when God shows us something new... a new direction He wants us to follow... a new ministry He wants us to start... or a new business He wants us to open, we lapse into amnesia. We forget that God has protected us, kept us, and blessed us in ways we never expected.

Thank God for His love and patience. Even after reassuring the disciples that He was not a ghost, Peter wanted more. He wanted a sign and Jesus gave him one. But, Peter stopped looking to Jesus and started looking at what was happening around him. He took his eyes off of Jesus for a split second, got scared, and started to sink. Peter was no different than we are. Even though Jesus was standing right there in front of him, Peter was still distracted by the circumstances surrounding him. But Jesus was well aware of the situation when He told Peter to step out of the boat and, "Come." Likewise, He knows our circumstances when He tells us to step out of our comfort zone, and do something.

He knows about the stack of unpaid bills; He knows about your wayward spouse; He knows about the trauma of your past; He knows about your trifling boss; and He knows that you're still grieving or heartbroken. But He also knows exactly what is required to change your situation. He knows how to turn your mourning into dancing.104 He knows how to turn your last dime into lights, heat, gas, water, and rent for a year.105 God wants you to Believe Bigger than your circumstances. He wants you to Believe Bigger than your fear and your doubt. When we trust Him, we are able to accomplish the impossible. But when we choose to focus on our circumstances, we will most certainly drown.

Think about this, if Bill Gates asked you to do something and promised to provide the financial backing for it, would you do it? Of course you would. It would be a no brainer. "Heck yeah!" You'd be an enthusiastic participant because Bill Gates is a billionaire. But have you ever seen Bill Gates' money? Have you personally looked at his balance sheets? Can you call up his bank right now and verify funds? Still, you would trust him at his word because of his reputation. You would trust him even though he's never done anything for you, personally. If anything, you've helped to bolster his bottom line by using his technology.

But when Jesus asks us to do something, and gives us assurance, we question it, want to pray about it, wonder if he really meant what He said. This faith journey will challenge you to increase your faith and take God at His word. If God has told you to take a step, you must focus your attention on Him and your assignment, and not on the storm around you. When Peter began to sink, he cried out, "Lord! Save Me!" and Jesus immediately reached down to rescue him. But He also asked a question that He's asking many of us today, "You have such little faith...why did you doubt?"

---

104 Psalm 30:11
105 See how God provided for a widow and her household in 1 Kings 17:8-16.

PRAY THIS

Lord I'm ready to step out of the boat. Help me to fix my gaze on you and not the storms around me. You make the impossible, possible. Give me the faith to believe. In Jesus Name, Amen.

TWEET | POST THIS

I'm ready to walk on water.
#BelievingBigger31

Believing Bigger: Why is it so hard to consistently trust God? What distractions or circumstances are getting in your way?

"Every mental act is composed of doubt and belief, but it is belief that is the positive, it is belief that sustains thought and holds the world together."
~ Soren Kierkegaard

25. DRY BONES

> *"And he said to me, 'Son of man, can these bones live?' And I answered, 'O Lord God, you know.'"*
> *Ezekiel 37:3*

In December 2014, I was at a particularly low point in my life. I was dealing with the strain of a troubled marriage, and it felt like no matter what I said, what I did, how much I prayed, or tried to keep my head up, there was just no hope. For the first time in a long time, I truly felt what it meant to be in despair. I felt the weight of failure. I was sinking in the mire of pity, and had neither the strength nor the inclination to pull myself out.

One Sunday, I found myself at church, but not really in church. I was physically present, but my mind was elsewhere.

I had no idea what the message was about and as I scrolled through the Bible on my tablet, I happened upon the 37th chapter of Ezekiel. I cried silent tears because I knew, right in that moment, God was speaking to me through His word, and telling me that everything was going to be alright.

Ezekiel 37 details a vision that God gave to the prophet Ezekiel. In the vision, Ezekiel finds himself in a Valley of Dry Bones. The bones represent a desolate wasteland, a place of despair, a place that was once vibrant and alive, but that had become dreary and deserted. No matter who you are, what you do, where you've been or where you're going, at some point in your life, you will encounter a Valley of Dry Bones. I encountered it in my marriage. Your Valley of Dry Bones might be in your career, your health, a close friendship, or death of a loved one. Whatever it is, at some point or another, we all find ourselves lost in a place where we don't know what to do or where to turn. And, in those moments, we likely wonder, Can these bones live?" In other words, we want to know will this ever stop hurting? Will I ever get through this? Am I ever going to recover? Is *happiness* still an option for me? Will I ever get this plan off the ground?

Sitting in church that day, the moment I read verses 5-6, real tears fell. God told Ezekiel to speak to the bones and say, "Behold, I will cause breath to enter you, and you shall live. And I will lay sinews upon you, and will cause flesh to come upon you, and cover you with skin, and put breath in you, **and you shall live**, and you shall know that I am the Lord." When I saw the words, **"and you shall live,"** I knew that God was telling me that I was going to get through this, that I wouldn't always be as sad as I was in that moment. And He was right.

One year later, it's hard for me to believe that I was ever that sad. When God said that I would **live,** He didn't just mean that I would "survive." He meant that I would **LIVE**! I would be restored, healed, and revived. My *situation* did not change instantaneously, but my mindset did. And I can testify that if it had not been for God speaking to me through His word that day, I might have been clinically depressed or worse. When God delivers you from your *Valley* of Dry Bones, you will know that it was the Lord.

No one is exempt from the Valley of Dry Bones. Even the most revered leaders experience seasons of dryness. Look at Nelson Mandela; he spent nearly three decades in prison, isolated from the world, locked in a concrete cell alone. But he knew that his Valley was for but a season. His situation did not change overnight, but he held on to hope saying, "There were many dark moments when my faith in humanity was sorely tested, but I would not and could not give myself up to despair. That way lay defeat and death."

When God delivered Nelson Mandela from his Valley of Dry Bones in 1990, He didn't just let Mr. Mandela enjoy the next few years of his life peacefully tucked away in some unknown part of the universe. No, God elevated him to the president of his country, where he served a full term, was awarded the Nobel Prize and remained a beloved hero until his last breath in 2013. God breathed life into Mr. Mandela's situation and caused him to **LIVE!**

So, if you're wondering, like I was that day in church, whether your dry bones will live again, the answer is, "YES!" When the bones – which represented the Israelites, a devastated people destroyed by disobedience and ravaged by war and captivity – came together in Ezekiel's vision, they cried out, "Our bones are dried up, and our hope is lost; we are indeed cut off" (37:11). But God reassured them saying, "I will open your graves and raise you from your graves, O my people... And you shall know that I am the Lord... And I will put my Spirit within you, and **you shall LIVE...** Then you shall know that I am the Lord; **I have spoken, and I will do it**" (12-14 *emphasis* added.)

When you encounter your own Valley of Dry Bones, remember that God, the giver and sustainer of life,106 is also there with you.107 He knows the situation and knows how to cause the bones, sinews, and flesh to come together. And He will breath life back into you so that you may live. Jesus said, "I came that they might have life and have it abundantly."108 God said, "I have spoken, and I will do it."

---

106 Psalm 36:9
107 Psalm 23:4
108 John 10:10

PRAY THIS

Lord thank you for being with me in my valley of dry bones. Thank you for second chances and 30th chances. Thank you for grace and mercy that assures me that I WILL LIVE.

Amen

TWEET | POST THIS

God has spoken, and He will Do it.

#BelievingBigger31

Believing Bigger: Have you been through a Valley of Dry Bones? How did God bring you out? If you're currently in one, how is God speaking to you through this passage?

"There is no easy walk to freedom anywhere,
and many of us will have to pass through the valley of
the shadow of death again and again before we reach the
mountaintop of our desires."
~ Nelson Mandela

26. WAR

> *"Therefore put on the full armor of God, so that when the day of evil comes, you may be able to stand your ground, and after you have done everything, to stand."*
> Ephesians 6:13

I remember the first time I heard the words "spiritual warfare." I imagined angels and demons locked in an epic battle of good and evil, with Star Wars light sabers, warring for our souls. I understood the concept in theory, but the logical part of my brain didn't fully grasp it until a series of unfortunate events drove me to my knees like never before. In the span of three years, my marriage, my health, my mother's health, my daughter's health, my finances, and my walk with Christ started to crumble. To say that I was not prepared would be a gross understatement. I wasn't just ill prepared for the attack; I was ill prepared to fight!

In The Art of War, Sun Tzu warns:
If you know the enemy and know yourself, you need not fear the result of a hundred battles.
If you know yourself but not the enemy, for every victory gained you will also suffer a defeat. If you know neither the enemy nor yourself, you will succumb in every battle.

The enemy knew me. He had studied me. He had assessed my weaknesses, my vulnerabilities, my fears, and my frustrations. But I was so caught up in the "hustle and bustle" of life that I was completely oblivious until he attacked. And he didn't just strike in a single location, but had coordinated a series of simultaneous attacks that I was ill prepared to defend. The plan was not one that was hatched overnight. It was carefully planned; the enemy patiently waited, carrying on with seemingly normal daily activities until it was time to strike. This is how the devil works. He knows you, but if you don't take the time to understand who he is,

125

how he works, and how he will stalk you until he finds an area of weakness,[109] you will suffer defeat in battle, just like I did, and just like Sun Tzu warns. Let's consider his warning from a spiritual lens.

If you know the enemy and know yourself, you need not fear the result of a hundred battles.

When you know who you are in Christ, when you are confident of the gifts He has given you, when you have tested the equipment for battle (studying God's word), when you are honest about your weaknesses,[110] and clear that your enemy is waiting for an opportunity to strike, but know that God has already given you the victory,[111] then you do not need to fear the outcome.

You know that the result of the battle means nothing because the **war** has already been won.

If you know yourself but not the enemy, for every victory gained you will also suffer a defeat.

When you are blind or naive to the fact that the devil is constantly looking for an opportunity to expose your weaknesses, then no matter how confident you are of your identity in Christ, you leave yourself vulnerable to attack. This is what happened to me. I naively believed that going to church on Sundays, paying my tithes, serving in ministry, and volunteering for missions somehow exempted me from tribulation. What I didn't know at the time was that the more I served, the more likely I was to be attacked. Bishop Joseph Walker often says, that "dogs don't bark at parked cars." What he means is that the closer you get to your destiny in Christ, the more demonic forces you are likely to attract.

So while you may win some battles, you will also suffer in other areas, if you are not clear on the fact that you are in a fight.

---

109 1 Peter 5:8
110 2 Corinthians 12:9
111 2 Chronicles 2:17

If you know neither the enemy nor yourself, you will succumb in every battle.

In our dizzying world of emails, texts, tweets, live streams and more, many of us are so distracted that we don't take the time to pray, to read, to meditate on God's word, or recognize patterns of destruction. When you're so busy being busy, you are at the greatest risk of attack. Imagine a person so distracted by their cell phone that they overlook an upcoming manhole. YouTube is chock full of videos showing people who have fallen headfirst into fountains, crashed into light poles, or tripped over a curb because they were so busy looking down that they never saw the danger ahead.

Like those people, the enemy's job is to keep you looking down. He knows that if he can keep you bogged down with mindless distractions, overloaded with information, worried about work, and stressed by the chaos at home and the mess in the church, then you will be too tired, too irritated, too busy, and too bothered to equip yourself with the spiritual light saber you need to fight him.[112]

When I started paying attention, I realized that the enemy had been able to coordinate a sophisticated attack because my prayer life was severely lacking. Prayer is one of the most powerful weapons in our spiritual arsenal and I was underutilizing it. At the time of attack, I was waking up each morning and giving God a 5-second shout-out, but that was hardly enough to withstand the spiritual wickedness that the devil had in store. I needed a new game plan.

Your faith journey is going to require you to reevaluate your spiritual war strategy to determine if you are equipped for the fight. You will have to look at some of the spiritual battles you've won, as well as

---

112 Ephesians 6:13

the ones that wounded you. What were the casualties? What were the victories? What spiritual tools did you use to win? And what spiritual techniques do you need to include in your arsenal now. The enemy is at the gates. Are you ready for battle?

PRAY THIS

Lord, open my eyes to the traps and snares of the enemy. Equip me for battle with Your Word, put a hedge of protection around my heart and mind; and help me to stay committed to fighting in prayer.
Amen.

TWEET | POST THIS

Prayer + Praise makes the enemy behave.
#BelievingBigger31

Believing Bigger: What battles are you currently facing? What weapons are you using to fight? What areas of weakness might the enemy be exploiting?

"Know thyself. Know thy enemy. A thousand battles. A thousand victories."

~ Sun Tzu

27. LIAR LIAR

> *"… He was a murderer from the beginning, and does not stand in the truth, because there is no truth in him. When he lies, he speaks out of his own character, for he is a liar and the father of lies."John 8:44*

In September 2009, during his first year in office, President Obama delivered a speech to Congress outlying his plan for public health insurance. As he addressed concerns about whether his plan would cover illegal immigrants, Senator Joe Wilson of South Carolina leapt from his seat, pointed an accusatory finger, and shouted, "YOU LIE!" Though his congressional peers later rebuked him, the incident is known as one of the most egregious acts of disrespect by a congressman towards a sitting president. The audacity. The nerve. Regardless of whether Senator Wilson respected President Obama as a man, he was obligated, as a public servant, to respect President Obama's position.

Satan has no such obligation. He does not respect you as a person, and he certainly doesn't care about your position as child of God. When Satan tempted Jesus in the wilderness, he knew full well who Jesus was.[113] Jesus was God in human flesh, and had come to die for the sins of the world. Satan also knows that Jesus will eventually return to cast him into an eternal lake of fire.[114] Yet none of that prevented him from trying to catch Jesus off guard, and tempting Him at a time when he thought Jesus would be weak from fasting. In short, the devil has no chill. He takes no breaks, and there are no limits to how far he will go to destroy those who love the Lord. God's sovereign authority is the only thing that keeps the devil at bay. Satan literally has to request God's permission to attack

---

113 Matthew 4:1-11
114 Revelation 20:10

you.[115] But, that does not stop Satan from trying to take us out, and he has a number of tools at his disposal to help him. One of his favorite weapons of mass destruction is lying (John 8:44). While lying may not seem like much of a weapon, we must remember that a single, crafty lie was the catalyst that brought sin into the entire world.[116] We, clearly, underestimate the power of Satan's lies. But the real issue is not *that* Satan lies; it's that *we believe him*. Though he's been telling the same lies for millennia, we keep falling prey to them. Here are just a few of his lies:

It's hopeless.

If God really existed... such and such wouldn't have happened.

Sin isn't so bad; that's why it feels so good. God wants you to be happy right?

It's never going to happen for you.

You're not good enough.

You call yourself a Christian? Hypocrite.

You can't do it.

You are nothing without money and wealth.

Live for the moment (Carpe Diem!)

Do any of these sound familiar? I'm certain that you've heard at least one of these lies before, or at least one of its many variations. Satan doesn't fight fair. He's a master liar. So this faith journey is going to require you to fight fire with fire. The only thing that can destroy Satan's lies is God's truth. This is how Jesus defeated Satan in the wilderness and this is how you can defeat him too. So when Satan comes for you with any one of his favorite lies, hit him back with the truth from the Word of God. Commit these truths to memory, post them on your mirror, recite them when you're getting dressed in the morning. Call Satan out on his lies and let him know

---

115 Job 1:7-12; Luke 22:31
116 Genesis 3:1-5

that his time is up.

PRAY THIS

Lord, thank you for equipping me with the tools to fight lies from the enemy. Help me to hide them in my heart and allow the Holy Spirit to recall them to my memory when I need them. In Jesus Name, Amen.

TWEET | POST THIS

The devil is a LIAR.
#BelievingBigger31

Satan's Lies	God's Truth
It's hopeless.	"The righteous cry out, and the Lord hears them; he delivers them from all their troubles. The Lord is close to the brokenhearted and saves those who are crushed in spirit. The righteous person may have many troubles, but the Lord delivers him from them all." **Psalms 34:17-19**
If God really existed... such and such wouldn't have happened.	"I will never leave you, nor forsake you." **Hebrews 13:5** "Count it all joy, my brothers, when you meet trials of various kinds, for you know that the testing of your faith produces steadfastness. And let steadfastness have its full effect, that you may be perfect and complete, lacking in nothing. **James 1:2-4**
Sin isn't so bad; that's why it feels so good. God wants you happy right?	"There is a way that seems right to a man, but its end is the way of death." **Proverbs 14:12** For the wages of sin is death, but the free gift of God is eternal life in Christ Jesus our Lord." **Romans 6:23**
It's never going to happen for you.	"Wait for the Lord; be strong, and let your heart take courage; wait for the Lord!" **Psalms 27:14** "Let us not become weary in doing good; for at the proper time we will reap a harvest if we do not give up." **Galatians 6:9**
You're not good enough.	"I will praise you because I am fearfully and wonderfully made." **Psalms 139:14**
You call yourself a Christian? Hypocrite. God will never forgive you for that.	"If we confess our sins, he is faithful and just to forgive us our sins and to cleanse us from all unrighteousness." **1 John 1:9**
You are nothing without material wealth	"Do not lay up for yourselves treasures on earth, where moth and rust destroy and where thieves break in and steal, but lay up for yourselves treasures in heaven... For where your treasure is, there your heart will be also." **Matthew 6:19-21**
Live for the moment.	"Be very careful, then, how you live— not as unwise but as wise, making the most of every opportunity, because the days are evil. Therefore do not be foolish, but understand what the Lord's will is." **Ephesians 5:15-17**

Believing Bigger: What lie is the devil trying to get you to believe? Which of God's truths can you use to combat it?

"A lie can travel halfway around the world, while the truth is still putting on its shoes."
~ Charles Spurgeon

28. MORE ABUNDANTLY

> *"The thief comes only to steal and kill and destroy. I came that
> they may have life and have it abundantly."*
> John 10:10

"And the Grinch, with his Grinch-feet ice cold in the snow,
stood puzzling and puzzling, how could it be so?
It came without ribbons. It came without tags.
It came without packages, boxes or bags.
And he puzzled and puzzled 'till his puzzler was sore.
Then the Grinch thought of something he hadn't before.
What if Christmas, he thought, doesn't come from a store.
What if Christmas, perhaps, means a little bit more."
Dr. Seuss, <u>How the Grinch Stole Christmas</u>

Over the past decade, the holidays have been a struggle for me.
I never thought I would be one of those people who suffer from
holiday blues, but I was. It is no coincidence that at a time when
I should have been rejoicing over the birth of our Savior, I found
myself feeling melancholy and out of sorts.

Instead of celebrating the gift of Christ, I found myself caught up in
the commercialization of Christmas. Instead of being a season of
joyous reflection, the holidays seemed to highlight how broke I was,
the things I couldn't afford, and the resentment I had built up for
having to buy gifts when I desperately needed to use that money
for bills or other necessities.

One of Satan's favorite places to attack is the mind, and I couldn't
shake that nagging voice in my head telling me that I was a failure
if I couldn't afford to buy a Keurig, iPhone, or the latest Ugg boots.
I felt pangs of inadequacy when friends and family bought gifts for
my child that I couldn't afford, instead of appreciating the blessing
of people who loved us enough to make provisions. And, social

media compounded the issue with its endless display of material wealth and status symbols reminding me of the life I thought I'd be able to afford by then. Though I gave lip service to Jesus being the Reason for the Season, inside I battled with discontent.

Looking back now, it seems foolish, but that's how the enemy works. The devil knows our weaknesses, insecurities, childhood hurts and pressure points, and will use those hurts to hurt us more. While God uses life's challenges and trials to manifest His glory, Satan tries to use those same situations to destroy us, and our relationship with Christ. This is because, from the moment you admit you are a sinner, believe that Jesus is the Son of God, and confess Him as Lord and Savior of your life, three things happen simultaneously: you receive the gift of eternal life, you receive the power of the Holy Spirit, and you become a target for the devil and his followers. Jesus came to give, but the devil exists to steal, kill, and destroy; and, he won't stop; he can't. Unlike the Grinch who came around just at Christmastime, the devil is busy at Christmas, Easter, Monday, Hump Day, all day, morning, noon, and night (#TeamNoSleep). He thrives on our misery and unhappiness.

Unfortunately, sometimes we aid him in his process of destruction. Think about it. When was the last time you really wanted something, but for whatever reason, were unable to get it? I don't mean, "Man...I really wanted cake, but I'll settle for these carrot sticks." I'm talking about a desperate desire: to have a child, to be debt free, to find a new job, to be in a happy relationship, to join an exclusive group, win a competition, or buy a house. When the things we desperately desire elude us, our feelings of disappointment easily turn into bitterness, envy, or disbelief in God's ability to provide. When we harbor resentment towards God and others, we become vulnerable prey for the enemy. A fleeting moment of disappointment is one thing, but when ships come to harbor, they drop anchor, and some of us have allowed bitter feelings to be anchored in our spirit.

That's exactly when the devil loves to strike. Just like sharks that attack when they smell blood, the devil knows that when you're already down, you'll likely be too weak to fight back.

But, the apostle Paul teaches us a great lesson about contentment and peace. In his letter to the church at Philippi, Paul wrote, "I know how to live on almost nothing or with everything. I have learned the secret of living in every situation, whether it is with a full or empty stomach, with plenty or little. For I can do everything through Christ who gives me strength."[117] Paul tells us that the secret to experiencing peace during any of life's circumstances is total and complete reliance on Jesus Christ. When we focus on the strength, wisdom, and provision we receive through faith in our Savior, it is easy to realize that Jesus is the gift that keeps on giving and that His love will outlast any flat screen TV, handbag, appliance, gizmo or gadget.

That is enough to make you shout! But, even in our moments of disappointment, we should still, like the Who's from Whoville, sing praises, lift our hands in worship, keep coming to church, keep tithing, keep trusting, and keep testifying to God's goodness because it will increase our faith and repel Satan like bug spray. If there is one thing the devil cannot stand, it's seeing you praise God anyhow. If there is one thing that will confuse and perplex him, it is seeing you continue to live with peace and contentment after one of his raids on your spirit. Our praises to God are like nails on a chalkboard for him, and the Word promises that if we resist him, he will flee from us.[118]

In this faith journey, you will experience periods of disappointment

117 Philippians 4:12-13 New Living Translation
118 James 4:7

from being unable to obtain certain desires. You may even struggle with wanting more of this or more of that. But, you must come to understand that true abundance does not come from what we have; it comes from who we are in Christ Jesus.

PRAY THIS

Lord, thank you for true abundance: of mercy, of grace, of forgiveness, of protection, of provision, of peace, of joy, and of love. These things have no price. Help me to never lose sight of that. In Jesus Name,
Amen.

TWEET | POST THIS

Having more doesn't come from a store. #BelievingBigger31

Believing Bigger: Have you fallen victim to materialism and over consumption? What things can you get rid of to start freeing yourself? What non-material things in your life do you truly value?

"Materialism is an identity crisis."
~ Bryant McGill

29. LIFE AND DEATH

> "'Lord,' Martha said to Jesus, 'if you had been here, my brother
> would not have died.'"
> John 11:21

Two things that make it hard for us to hold on to our faith and keep Believing Bigger are tragedy and loss. And few things cause more heartache, sadness, depression, and pain than death. Regardless of whether it's the death of a loved one, the death of a dream, or the death of a relationship, the pain grips us, consumes us, and makes it difficult to move forward. The head of the Grief Ministry at my church explains these feelings of grief as "the price we pay for love." But sometimes when we begin to experience such grief and such despair, we turn our feelings outward and become angry at God:

"You knew what that person meant to me. How could you?"

"Really God? You took away the one person that gave me hope?"

"If you loved me, you would never want me to hurt this badly."

We see a similar retort directed to Jesus when his dear friend, Lazarus, died.[119] Lazarus had been ill, and his sisters, Mary and Martha, sent desperate word to Jesus in hopes that Jesus would come and heal their brother. So many of us have done the same. When a loved one falls ill, when a marriage is on the rocks, when we're about to lose our homes or our jobs, we send desperate prayers to the Lord, praying that He will heal and restore. And we expect the Lord to respond...ASAP!

But, when Jesus found out that Lazarus was sick, he didn't hop on the first plane...er...donkey and ride out to his friend. In fact, He did the opposite. He intentionally waited for Lazarus to die and, even then, did not rush to comfort the sisters.

---

119 See John 11:1-44

You might be thinking, "Huh?!" Jesus had the power to prevent his friend's death, but He didn't. This was his a good friend, not some random stranger... If this had happened to you, would you be upset? Martha sure was. When Jesus arrived, Martha was *heated* and wasted no time letting Him know it. "Lord if you had been here, my brother would not have died!" She accused. Martha had a natural, emotional, *human* reaction. But let's examine these events through a spiritual lens.

Oftentimes we wrongly assume that Jesus isn't aware that our loved one, our dream, our marriage is on life-support. But He's well aware and knew it long before you did. So, then, why would He allow it? There are a variety of reasons God permits such things to occur – to draw us closer to Him, to help us grow, to teach us when it's time to release. Regardless of the reason, Paul tells us that *all things* work together for our good.[120] So we know that there is a purpose even in our most painful trials.

Consider this example. When a tree is pruned, certain branches or stems are removed in order to benefit the **whole tree**. Damaged and diseased branches have to be taken away in order to keep the decay from compromising the overall health of the tree. And our lives are the same. Sometimes things must be cut away in order for us to grow or thrive. It doesn't mean that those things are necessarily bad, it just means that our spiritual, mental, emotional, and physical health are hindered by the presence of that person or thing. And sometimes, we just need to be pruned, shaped, molded, before we can go to the next level. So God intervenes and shaves away some activities, some persons, some environments that have prevented us from rising to our full potential.

Other times, the most merciful thing to do is to let something or

---

120 Romans 8:28

someone go. How many of us have stayed in relationships that should have ended years ago? Or, when loved ones get stricken with cancer or worse, it's heartbreaking watching them suffer. Just because something is alive doesn't mean it's *living*. So though painful, sometimes we have to look beyond what's best for us, and instead at what's best for everyone. In Lazarus' case, Jesus had every intention of restoring Lazarus, but not for his sake or his sisters' sake, but so that *others* would believe in God (#ItsNotAboutYou). Jesus' own death on the cross was not in his personal best interest. At any moment, Jesus could have changed his mind and reigned on earth as King. But his concern was not for himself, but for us and to do the will of God.

Death and loss are never easy. But we can take comfort in knowing that, just as Jesus commanded Lazarus to rise, He can also speak life into our dying situations, whether it is our health, marriage, finances or future. And even in those times where death or loss is permanent, we can be assured that God can and will use the circumstances for our good because we know that God's intentions toward us are always to prosper us and not to harm us.[121]

121 Jeremiah 29:11

PRAY THIS

Lord, thank you for the revelation that sometimes in order for us to grow, we have to learn to let go. Lord, you know what's best for me, even though it may be painful. Sustain me through the hurt and the loss. In Jesus Name,
Amen.

TWEET | POST THIS

If I want to Grow, I have to Let Go.
#BelievingBigger31

Believing Bigger: What painful losses have you suffered? Surrender your hurt to God and pray for the wisdom to accept His will, His grace, and His peace.

"Some people are so afraid to die that they never begin to live."
~ Henry Van Dyke

30. BLOCKED CALL

> *"And when you stand praying, if you hold anything against anyone, forgive them, so that your Father in heaven may forgive you your sins."*
> Mark 11:25

If you ask people to name the single, greatest invention of the technological age, most would say computers, the Internet, or perhaps cell phones. But if I had to cast a vote, I would give caller ID some major consideration. Since none of us have psychic powers, knowing who's on the other side of a ringing phone is a major asset, and helps us to anticipate what the caller might want. For example, if you have a cousin that only calls when she needs money, seeing her number on caller ID helps you decide whether to accept the call. Or, think about working adults who don't make a habit of answering their cell phones during work hours. Seeing the number from their child's school or the doctor's office might prompt them to make an exception. But, my favorite function of caller ID is being able to ignore calls from numbers that I don't recognize. I am notorious for this, especially when the caller ID reads: PRIVATE, UNKNOWN, or BLOCKED. If I see one of those three words, the caller may as well hang it up because I refuse to answer. Fortunately, God is not like me. For one thing, there are no PRIVATE calls to the Lord; He knows *exactly* who you are. After all, He created you.[122] Second, there is nothing UNKNOWN to God, absolutely nothing is hidden from Him.[123] However, there are ways we can BLOCK the chances of God answering the prayer line. One of the biggest myths about being a Christian is that God is only concerned about what we **do**. The whole truth is that God is also concerned about who we **are**. In other words, God doesn't limit His

---

122 Jeremiah 1:5
123 Hebrews 4:13

concern to whether you obey His commands. He is also concerned about the condition of our hearts. Jesus taught us this in the Gospel of Mark. While instructing his followers on prayer, Jesus cautioned them to pray with the right spirit, which included believing that God will answer your prayer and having a heart of forgiveness.[124] Sometimes trusting that God will answer our prayers is hard. But, forgiving someone is one of the most *excruciatingly difficult* things we have to do in life. Yet, it is still an **absolutely necessary** component to our faith. Sometimes we feel indignant about forgiving others. We don't think they deserve it and would rather punish them with silence, the cold shoulder, severed relationships, or by cursing them out, on social media or in front of the kids. But, how can we refuse to forgive someone else when none of us deserves God's forgiveness?[125] God doesn't owe it to us; but, He loves us and His forgiveness is a manifestation of that love.[126] That's why anytime we approach our loving God with an unloving spirit of bitterness and refusal to forgive, He will not hear us. In choosing not to forgive, you block your access *to* God, as well as block your blessings *from* God. Imagine the number of prayers that go unanswered because of unforgiving hearts. I can't speak for you, but I when I call on God, I need Him to answer. Even King David, with all of his fame, power, riches, and flaws too, knew how important it was to approach God with the right spirit. He wrote, "If I regard wickedness in my heart, the Lord will not hear [me]."[127] He knew that he couldn't fool God. Likewise, others might believe your fake smiles, Facebook posts, and going through the motions, but God is continually examining your **heart**.

Forgiveness is necessary. Why? It frees us and it frees the person(s)

---

124 Mark 11:24-25
125 Romans 3:23-28
126 Romans 5:8
127 Psalm 66:18 New American Standard Bible

who hurt us. This is also what makes forgiving so hard. If we're honest, we don't want the offender to "go free." That's not our idea of *justice*. That's not *fair*. But how fair was it for Jesus to get beaten in your place? How fair was it for Him to die for *your* sins?

The Bible says that Jesus knew no sin, but became sin out of obedience to God.[128] The King of Kings and Lord of Lords was publicly humiliated and persecuted for us. Was that *justice*? No. It was LOVE.

So, whenever we decide to play "god" instead of extending the same grace that God has extended to us, we demonstrate a lack of faith. We show that we don't trust God to exact justice on our behalf,[129] or to handle the matter properly. But when we extend the same mercy, grace, and forgiveness that He does, we unlock ourselves from a prison of bitterness, and unblock our access to God who is always willing to answer our call.[130]

PRAY THIS

Lord, thank You for forgiving me for my sins. Thank You for reminding me that the strength of my relationship with You depends on my reliance upon You to do the things that are hard for me to do in the flesh, like forgive. Soften my hard heart. In your name, Amen.

TWEET | POST THIS

When I pray, I need God to Answer on the first ring.
I will NOT let an unforgiving heart block my calls.
#BelievingBigger31

---

128 2 Corinthians 5:21
129 Romans 12:19
130 Psalm 34:4

Believing Bigger: Is there someone that you need to forgive? Who is it? Write down their name, what they did, and pray for them. Pray that God release you from bitterness and anger, and trust Him.

"It's one of the greatest gifts you can give yourself, to forgive. Forgive everybody."
~ Maya Angelou

31. IT'S TIME TO GET UP

> *"The sick man answered him, 'Sir, I have no one to put me into the pool when the water is stirred up, and while I am going another steps down before me.'"*
> John 5:7

Have you ever been sick for a prolonged period of time? Perhaps it was a bad cough or bug that just wouldn't go away. Maybe you sprained some part of your body, and the soreness ached on for months, even years. Right now, you might be living with physical limitations that hinder your ability to move around as much as you'd like. Or, it may even be that you were hurt emotionally, mentally, or psychologically, and the wounds linger on. Whether the ailment is physical or emotional, many of us have become accustomed to living with pain. And that was the situation for the men and women laying near the Pool of Bethesda.

In John, Chapter 5,[131] we encounter a scene of pain and desperation, as a multitude of sick people lay next to the pool, each one of them either blind, paralyzed, or badly limping.

The multitude lay there, hurting and helpless, waiting for an opportunity to be healed. As Jesus passed by, one man stood out. This particular man had been crippled for 38 years! Thirty-eight! Knowing his condition, He asked the man, "Do you want to get well?" (John 5:6). Instead of seizing the moment and answering with an emphatic, "YES! I absolutely do!" The man started telling Jesus about his problems. "The sick man answered Him, 'Sir, I have no man to put me into the pool when the water is stirred up, and while I am going another steps down before me'" (5:7).

Some of us, like this man, have been managing pain for so long that we don't recognize the opportunity for healing right in front of

---

131 John 5:2-9

us. We don't hear Jesus asking us, **"Do you want to get well?"** We have gotten so used to complaining, so used to the bitterness, so used to disappointment, that we become like the people at the Pool of Bethesda: blind, paralyzed, and badly limping. For 38 years, this man sat on the sidelines, watching others get healed, receive breakthroughs, and walk away happy and whole. But, he was so blinded by years of disappointment that he didn't even recognize that his healing had arrived. Jesus was standing right before him. At this point in your faith journey, you have to answer the questions, "Do I want to get well?" "Am I ready to be healed?" When Jesus questioned the man, He got excuses in return. Maybe it was because healing meant that the man would have no more reasons, no more excuses not to live his life full out. Are you like that man? Is your pain keeping you from living full out? Are the years of built up disappointment, frustration, and doubt holding you back? Are you so focused on the *illness* in your life that you don't see the cure, Jesus, standing right in front of you?

While it is true that pain serves a purpose, there is a measured start and end time for it. Pain helps us identify, where there is an injury, or a wound in need of healing. And the process of removing pain can teach us patience, humility, compassion, empathy, and gratitude. But when pain has finished its work, we become liberated to do a greater work, a more meaningful work. Thousands of people have benefited from their painful moments in life. They have used those experiences as rays of light for other people. They turned their misery into their ministry and their heartbreak into hope for others. And Jesus did the same for us. He came, as God in flesh, to live among us, to understand our temptations, our disappointments, and our hurts. But, His suffering, His painful experiences ended on the cross. And now, He continues to do meaningful work for us, interceding on our behalf.

At the Pool of Bethesda, Jesus told the crippled man, "Get up, take up your bed, and walk," and immediately the man was healed (5:8-9). Likewise, Jesus is telling you to "**get up**." Whatever pit you've been in, **get up**. Whatever pain you've been holding on to, **get up**. Whatever hurt you've been feeling, **get up**. Whatever bitterness you've been harboring, **get up**. Whatever doubts you've been having, **GET UP!** Take up your bed – your excuse, your past, your disappointment – and walk!

Now is the time for you to move *forward*. Your journey to Believing Bigger has just begun. You've taken an important first step, but you must stay in motion. The enemy will never stop attacking, but the God in you is greater than anything the devil can throw your way.[132] He is defeated; you are victorious. He is conquered, but you are a conqueror. He is a liar, but you know the Truth and the Truth has made you free.[133] This is your time. Seize it! GET UP!

132 1 John 4:4
133 John 8:32

PRAY THIS

Father God, thank You for healing me.
Thank You for restoring me.
Thank You, for showing me that my pain has a purpose.
Help me to Believe Bigger. Lead me to a greater work.
Empower me to Answer the Call. I want to be made whole.
I want to get up. Help me take up every excuse and live the life
You are calling me to live.
In Jesus Name,
Amen.

TWEET | POST THIS

This is my season. It's time to GET UP and GET TO WORK!
#BelievingBigger31

Believing Bigger: What do you need to pick so that you can walk freely and live full out? Are you ready to be healed?

Comeback is a good word, man.
~ Mickey Rourke

EPILOGUE YES AND AMEN

"For no matter how many promises God has made, they are 'Yes' in Christ. And so through him the 'Amen' is spoken by us to the glory of God."
2 Corinthians 1:20

Have you ever known a "sometime-y" person? This is the kind of person whose spirit is up one day and down the next. People like this may act like your best friend one week and the next time you see them, have barely two words to say to you. You can't depend on them because you never know what you're going to get. They commit to come to your birthday celebration or housewarming, but never show. They promise to help offset your child's prom expenses, but never deliver. They agree to send you the contact information for a job lead, but don't follow through, even after several reminders. Whether the commitment is large or small, these time wasters, promise breakers, and fakers make it virtually impossible to establish credibility.   Thankfully, Jesus is not like that. Paul writes that no matter how many promises God has made, they are always a Yes in Christ.[134] When we accepted Christ as Savior, we were adopted into God's family[135] and God always keeps his promises to his children.[136] God does not renege. He does not promise us things and then not deliver. And he is not slow in fulfilling His promises.[137]

---

134 2 Corinthians 2:21
135 Romans 8:17
136 Deuteronomy 7:9; Psalm 145:13
137 2 Peter 3:9

The Bible is filled with thousands of God's promises and we can count on every single one of them. Let's look at a few:

God Promises Salvation to the Believer	*Romans 1:16-17*
God Promises to Work in Our Best Interests	*Romans 8:28*
God Promises to Comfort Us in Times of Grief	*2 Corinthians 1:3-4*
God Promises a New Life free from the Guilt of our Past	*Romans 8:1-4; 2 Corinthians 5:17*
God Promises to Forgive Us When We Mess Up	*1 John 1:9*
God Promises to Supply All of Our Needs	*Philippians 4:19*
God Promises to Receive Us in Heaven	*John 14:1-3*

Your faith journey will have no shortage of obstacles, challenges, and discouragement. But the race is not won by the swift or the strong,[138] but by the one who endures until the end.[139] In Christ, we have the victory. All of the promises of God are Yes and all we have to say is, "Amen!"

---

138 Ecclesiastes 9:11
139 Matthew 24:13

Contact Info

To book Dr. Shante for Speaking and Teaching
Engagements, visit: Drshantesays.com/contact

Social Media

Twitter and Instagram, @DrShanteSays,
or on Facebook, fb.com/drshantesays

Website

www.believingbigger.com

Faith Summit Registration

Join Dr. Shante to for a full day of faith,
fuel, and freedom to live your

calling at the Believing Bigger Faith Summit

REGISTER at www.BelieveBiggerSummit.com